Torn Asunder

Also by David H. Rosen

Children's Books

Henry's Tower
Time, Love and Licorice: A Healing Coloring Storybook
Samantha the Sleuth & Zack's Hard Lesson
Kindergarten Symphony: An ABC Book

Poetry

The Healing Spirit of Haiku (With Joel Weishaus)
Clouds and More Clouds
Spelunking through Life
Living with Evergreens
In Search of the Hidden Pond
White Rose, Red Rose(With Johnny Baranski)
Torii Haiku: Profane to a Sacred Life
Look Closely
Warming to Gold
Every Day is a Good Day

Historical Fiction and Memoir

Opal Whiteley's Beginning and Hoops & Hoopla
Lost in the Long White Cloud: Finding My Way Home

Non-Fiction

Lesbianism: A Study of Female Homosexuality (1st edition)
Medicine as a Human Experience (With David Reiser)
Transforming Depression: Healing the Soul through Creativity
The Tao of Jung: The Way of Integrity
The Tao of Elvis
Patient-Centered Medicine: A Human Experience (With Uyen Hoang)
The Alchemy of Cooking: Recipes with a Jungian Twist
Lesbianism : A Father-Daughter Conversation (With Rachel Rosen)

Fay Book Series in Analytical Psychology

Editor and author of the forewords for the first 20 volumes of the Fay Book Series in Analytical Psychology. See the Appendix for a complete listing of these Fay books.

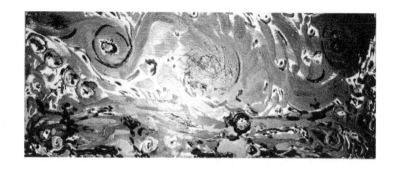

Torn Asunder

Putting Back the Pieces

a Memoir

BY DAVID H. ROSEN

RESOURCE *Publications* · Eugene, Oregon

TORN ASUNDER
Putting Back the Pieces: a Memoir

Resource Publications
An Imprint of Wipf and Stock Publishers
199 W. 8th Ave., Suite 3
Eugene, OR 97401

www.wipfandstock.com

PAPERBACK ISBN: 978-1-7252-8629-0
HARDCOVER ISBN: 978-1-7252-8628-3
EBOOK ISBN: 978-1-7252-8630-6

Manufactured in the U.S.A.   11/23/20

For my best friend and wife, Lanara Sophia Emmanuel Rosen

Who can find a good woman?
She is precious beyond all things.
Her husband's heart trusts her completely.
She is his best reward.

—PROVERBS 31:10–11

Disclaimer

While all of the incidents in this book are true, some of the names and personal characteristics of the individuals involved have been changed. For years I have recorded daily life in journals, and the data in this memoir is a faithful rendering of events from those pages.

Contents

Acknowledgements

I thank and deeply appreciate everyone who is a part of this book; especially my three daughters, Sarah, Laura, and Rachel, my two grandsons, Aidan and Ben, my siblings, Janet, Bill, Marti, and Nancy, my former wives, Lynn and Deborah (Debbie), goddaughter Annahita and my parents, Barbara and Max Rosen, who made it all possible. As always, soulful thanks to Lanara. I feel deep gratitude to Bonnie Sheehey and Rebekah Sinclair, who provided editorial assistance. And, heartfelt thanks to James Stock, Jim Tedrick, and staff at Wipf & Stock publishers for another outstanding job.

Illustrations

(All artwork is by the author, except where noted)

Epigraphs

Thou canst not be hewn asunder, for Thou indeed but one.

—MICHELANGELO

When the world falls in around you, you have pieces to pick up.

—NAOMI SHIHAB NYE

The best way to predict the future is to create it.

—ABRAHAM LINCOLN

Moving Toward Wholeness

Preface

Knowing others is intelligence;
knowing yourself is true wisdom.
Mastering others is strength;
mastering yourself is true power.

If you realize that you have enough,
you are truly rich.
If you stay in the center
and embrace death with your whole heart,
you will endure forever.

—Lao Tzu

My *daimon* is writing. Writing is who I am, and is a way of putting back the pieces. I once dreamt of the poet Wallace Stevens and his illness. He also wrote to heal himself. This memoir is a way for a wounded physician to tell about being torn apart and putting back the pieces. This book picks up where my last one ended, and covers my middle years from ages 30 to 60 (1975–2005).[1]

---

1. My first memoir, *Lost in the Long White Cloud: Finding My Way Home*, covered conception to the death of my father (from birth to age 30). See Rosen, D.H. (2014). *Lost in the Long White Cloud: Finding My Way Home*. Eugene, OR: Wipf & Stock.

I am now seventy five. The Buddhist religious scholar Gempo Yamamoto was right: at seventy, one feels more useful. However, as I write these words, I am also dealing with all that comes with having MS. My personal journey with this condition has been long and mysterious. It took a while to be diagnosed. Walking with Lanara in the Texas heat in 2007, my left leg was wobbly. Oh, we thought, a tired leg. I fell up a set of stairs shortly thereafter (which is rather hard to do, but is much better than falling down them), and ended up spilling a cup of coffee just before a student's dissertation defense. So I got a cane, thinking it was an old L4-L5 disc injury. Then my mother died. This loss was very depressing, painful, and very stressful. On the way to her memorial service, I developed double vision, which led to never driving again. At the time, I thought this was related to severe grief over my mother's death and chronic migraine headaches. But, I knew something was awry. I finally found out what my condition was on the day I married Lanara (December 17, 2009). After numerous tests, my neurologist, Dr. Joan Jensen, calmly said that I had "sclerosis." I asked, "What?" She responded, "Scars. You have multiple sclerosis." When she looked at my stunned face, she added, "This is not a death sentence. There are treatments." I looked in her eyes and asked, "Physician to physician, what would you do?" She said, "I would take Copaxone." "Okay," I answered, "please write a prescription." When I went to the pharmacy, I received a three month supply. The cost was more than $3,000. The pharmacist asked, "Do you still want it?" I gave him my insurance card. He phoned in the insurance and said, "That will be $70." This experience points out the moral issue involved in health care. In other words, health care ought to be a right of all citizens.

In addition to writing, I also cope with tragedy by doing comedy. When doing standup, I use the name, Dr. Nada, which I realize is related to my inner angst.[2] Thank God and Sophia that I've never taken myself or life too seriously. However I do know that truth-telling is part of my character (it's also part of comedy).

2. See my standup performance, Dr. Nada Live at the Tiny Tavern at https://www.youtube.com/watch?v=0TUSNrU7f7A.

So the following quote from John 8:32 rings true, "the truth shall set you free."

In 1975, when this book begins, I had just become a young faculty member at the Langley Porter Institute, which is the Psychiatry Department at the University of California, San Francisco Medical Center (UCSF). I had received a grant, "The Shetland Health Study," from the NIMH (National Institute of Mental Health), written with my then-wife, Deborah Voorhees-Rosen, and Richard Suzman. Receiving a significant grant made others envious. My introverted nature was heightened. However, I had good models of extroverted faculty whom I worked with, such as Mardi Horowitz, who became a mentor and academic model. He was an artist and physician-scientist, as I am. I therefore felt him to be a kindred spirit in a strange land.

Being a new faculty member can be difficult. Soon after arriving at UCSF, the department head put me in charge of the least desirable position at the institution: I was the Psychiatry representative to the Committee on Committees. When he threw me under the bus and I asked him about this position, he said, "I don't know what this is, but it must be important." As it turned out, it was a committee consisting of the oldest professors (deadwood) and all the youngest, undistinguished professors (fresh wood) of all the departments at the institution.

The opening of this book includes a peak experience: writing a grant, having it funded, and moving to Shetland with my then-wife, Debbie. At that time, so happy with my life, my work, and my wife, I had no idea that later, she would break my heart. A large part of this book is spent recounting how I tried to pick up and put back the pieces after a traumatic divorce.
But this, too, would be an important part of my journey in learning that broken hearts can mend.

As I tell my own story, I know that the truth of the events therein were perceived differently by each person. Truth is multifaceted. However, history has a way of putting together the pieces. Loren Eiseley, author of *The Immense Journey*, outlined a meaningful process in his memoir. It is not easy to write; it's complicated.

An autobiography involves courage and risk. One has to come up with all the pieces as the puzzle image slowly emerges.

Torn Asunder: Putting Back the Pieces is connected to the German word used by William James, "Zerissenheit," which means "torn-to-pieces-ness."[3] This memoir contains dreams and experiences that I recorded in journals. I offer up these stories - which sometimes seemed to write themselves - in the hope that they will be helpful to and embolden others. And, it has allowed me to actualize my personal myth of a wounded healer who writes to heal.

As Wallace Stevens once knew, "There is a poem in the heart of things." Throughout the memoir, you will see my love of small poems, many of which are haiku. They speak of my stories and feelings as well as anything. Also, since I am a Jungian Psychoanalyst, I really like dreams, and open each chapter by recounting a dream I had in the year I'm writing about, followed by a little analysis of its significance.

I close this preface with a guiding message from the Jewish sage, Hillel: "If I am not concerned for myself, who will be for me? But, if I am only concerned for myself, what good am I? And if now is not the time to act, when will it be?"

---

3. Richardson, R.D. (2006). *William James: In the Maelstrom of American Modernism: A Biography*. Boston: Houghton Mifflin.

Chapter 1: Rebirth in the Shetland Isles

Yesterday is history, tomorrow is a mystery, and today is a gift.

—ELEANOR ROOSEVELT

I dreamt that I was in a softball game, hit a triple and drove in two runs. It was a positive feeling being a member of a team.

Getting a grant funded is like hitting a triple and scoring two runs. And, it was affirmative being a member of a research team.

I then dreamt of my father. *He looked good and healthy, but then he turned grey and pale. After that he fell and I had to take him to the hospital. "Oh father!" Then he died.*

My dream-father dying represents the healing that occurs in the unconscious. Having the chance to be with him again before he died is like passing the baton from my outer to my inner authority.

When I turned thirty on February 25, 1975, I wrote in my journal, "It feels like a turning-point." I had just started seeing a Freudian analyst for help with very my deep anger issues, my challenges in relationships, and my trauma surrounding my parents, who had a very difficult and trying relationship. As you will see throughout this memoir, my anger issues resurface time and again, as do my problems with relationships. Watching parents trapped in unloving and resentful marriage did not set me up well to have my own healthy relations. My mother was a social worker, and my father was a war injured physician. They both were very loving and responsible parents, overcoming a lot in order to both work and support a family, but their love for each other lessened over time. Recognizing the source of my anger and relational issues while in therapy and later analysis is what prompted me to become an analyst myself.

Over the summer we lived and worked with another couple, Barbara and Gary Lapid, in order to carry out the baseline research for the project. We were interested in seeing whether Shetland's collective identity and unique approach to North Sea oil limited the negative effects on their way of life. The United States Department of Health, Education and Welfare (National Institute of Mental Health) funded our longterm *Shetland Health Study* from 1975–1981. We interviewed hundreds of subjects on the main island, both in the target region near Sullom Voe (which became Europe's largest oil port), and on the West side near Sandness, a conservation region that served as a control group. We later published our findings.[1]

Our life in Shetland was precious, as we were settlers. We learned to use a tusker and cut peat. After it dried, we burned it in our fireplace and stove. The neighbors across the way brought eggs and we would give them oranges that we bought in Lerwick, the main city. It was incredibly windy. Sometimes I had to crawl and grab on to the ever-present heather or be blown over.

---

1. Rosen, D.H. and Voorhees-Rosen, D.J. (1978) "The Shetland Islands: The effects of social and ecological change on mental health." *Culture, Medicine, and Psychiatry,* 2: 41–67; Rosen, David H., Voorhees, Deborah J. and Suzman, Richard M. "Shetland and North Sea Oil: A study of rapid social change and health—a three-year follow-up" in *The New Shetlander,* 1978.

Chapter 1: Rebirth in the Shetland Isles

Look closely. . .
wind blown
heather and me

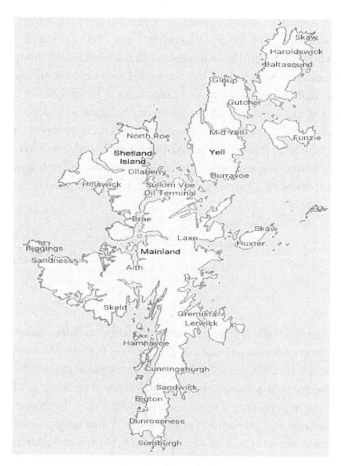

Map of the Shetland Isles

In mid June, Debbie and I ventured south to the mainland of Scotland, where we presented our research project to the Department of Psychiatry at the University of Edinburgh. After this, she stayed in Shetland and began the project. Before I returned to San Francisco where I worked, we made love. This led to the conception of our first daughter, Sarah.

In October of 1975, I met Debbie in London and we traveled on to Jerusalem, where I presented a paper at the Eighth International Congress on Suicide Prevention.[2] Yes, I was writing on suicide prevention. As they say, research is me-search, and though I have never been suicidal, I have struggled with depression. I agree with Teilhard de Chardin, that "humanity is being taken to the point where it will have to choose between suicide and adoration." At any rate, when we were in Israel, the Israeli security was so strict that they had a female official take Debbie aside and search her because of her pregnant belly. While there, like many other pilgrims, we experienced a special spiritual light. Jerusalem glowed as did my wife.

> "Many waters cannot quench love."
>
> —SONG OF SOLOMON 8:7

Since I had a full-time job as an academic, as chief resident in Psychiatry, I had to go back to San Francisco. But when I returned, I lived alone. Living in solitude had been a dream of mine. It suited me better than joining a monastery. I enjoyed working as chief resident in psychiatry. I was evaluated by faculty to determine if I was worthy to be a member of the faculty. I also taught an introductory course to medical students with Dr. Horowitz. Fortunately, there was an expectation that I do clinical work and research. I loved seeing patients, so that was a joy. What to research was answered when I picked up a *San Francisco Chronicle* one day and saw that a Stanford undergraduate student had jumped off the

---

2. Rosen, D.H. (1975). "Suicide Survivors: The Psychotherapeutic Implications of Egocide." Presented at the Eighth International Congress on Suicide Prevention. Jerusalem, Israel, October 21, 1975.

Golden Gate Bridge and survived. I found this unbelievable because I couldn't imagine that anyone could survive such a leap. This led to a project in which I initially researched six survivors, and later expanded to ten.[3] It turned out that each of the survivors had a religious experience, as described by William James in *The Varieties of Religious experience*

Starting left to right: Dr. Albert Hunter and his wife, Lena. Debbie and I. Dr. Gary Lapid and his wife, Barbara, who helped us gather baseline data in Shetland. In the background is Busta House-Hotel (which dates from 1588) where we were going for dinner. On the right is an old croft house.

3. Rosen, D.H. (1975). "Suicide Survivors: A Follow-Up Study of Persons Who Survive Jumping from the Golden Gate and San Francisco-Oakland Bay Bridges." *Western Journal of Medicine* 122: 289–294. See also Rosen, D.H. (1993). *Transforming Depression: A Jungian Approach Using the Creative Arts.* New York: Taucher/Putnam.

Chapter 2: Return to Academic Life

To write prescriptions is easy, but to come to an understanding of
people is hard.

—Franz Kafka

I dreamt I was on top of a mountain with a woman.

I realize now that the woman was my muse or anima. And, if a
man wants to know about his anima (feminine side), just look at
the woman he is with.

In 1975–1976, my wife and I spent a year in Shetland laying
the foundation for and beginning a huge research project, which
ended up lasting for several years. We were studying the impact
of establishing of rapid sole change on individual and communal
health. Europe's largest oil port was established in Solem Vole, before which the largest industry was a 20 person fish packing plant.
We thought the effects of rapid social change would be deleteri-
ous, but in fact, we found that accumulation of wealth seemed, at
least in the short term, to have a positive impact. The truth would
likely be more complicated if the study had continued today, and
we were able to track multigenerational change.

At the time, I was very close with my wife. While in Great
Britain, we visited London, we went to the Tate Gallery, where we

saw paintings by Van Gogh, Degas, Picasso, Chagall, and Matisse. All favorites of ours. I was feeling very positive and loving.

> God and Sophia hug. . .
> birds everywhere

Unfortunately, I once again had to return to my responsibilities in San Francisco. I had a frequently reoccurring and very debilitating headaches. I feared a brain tumor, and had thoughts of suicide. Perhaps this had to do with the pressures of being a chief resident and being separated from my wife. In any case, perhaps these struggles were in part what prompted me to grow beard and, more importantly, to take the step of caring for my own depression by seeing analysts.

Alex Simon, the head of Langley Porter, and I

Interestingly, beards are associated with depression and creativity. Abraham Lincoln and William James had beards, and they were prone to depressive episodes, as were Sigmund Freud and Leo Tolstoy.

Abraham Lincoln William James Sigmund Freud Leo Tolstoy

In 1975, I became a lecturer at UCSF, which started my academic career. I felt a deep kinship with William James, who also dealt with the issue of suicidal depression. Most likely that's the reason I read his books early on, as they connected to my research with survivors of jumps off the Golden Gate Bridge. James talks about the deadly jump "salto mortale" in *The Meaning of Truth*.[1] By carrying out both the Shetland Health Study, and the research around survivers from the Gold Gate Bridge, I was able, maybe for the first time, to name and recognize, even if not get beyond, my severe depression.

1. James, William. (1992) *The Meaning of Truth*. Cambridge, MA: Harvard University Press. (p.246–248)

My fondness for William James has helped me be a physician in the university. It was a comfort to know that James was also a medical doctor in a psychology department. It's always struck me that university relates to everything. The word has the universe in it. My continuing research has been like a tree branching out to many different fields and areas. I was comforted by James's multiple interests and delays in finishing work, as I was also slow at completing projects.

It is also noteworthy that I have always been troubled by abortion. In fact, I often find myself walking into Catholic churches. I was a colleague with Michael Peterson during residency. Michael was a psychiatrist who later became a Catholic priest. He founded St. Luke's Institute in Washington D.C. to treat priests and religious persons for drug and alcohol addictions. Like I always say, research is me-search. Michael was able to heal from his own addictions by helping others. As another example, while at the University of Rochester, I spent time at a Trappist monastery in Piffard, New York.

I enjoyed teaching and conducting research as part of my academic position. I was also fond of helping the mentally ill. Since many of my professors were psychoanalysts, including the head of Langley Porter, Dr. Robert Wallerstein (who took over when Dr. Simon retired), I became fascinated with in-depth therapies and psychoanalysis. I was impressed with their kindness and healing abilities.

During this year, Deborah and I continued working on the Shetland and North Sea Oil Study.

Our first daughter, Sarah, was born on March 15, 1976 in the Maternity Annex of the local hospital in Lerwick. This was by design, as they viewed having a child not as an illness, but as a natural process. Sarah was delivered by a midwife, and the obstetrician, true to what the word means, stood by. As a humanistic physician, I appreciate the view of childbirth as a normal event in one's life. Prior to Sarah's birth, the midwife and general practitioner came to our home to make sure everything was in order and to educate us as soon-to-be parents.

Sarah in 2013

River oak
swaying. . .
silence.

Chapter 3: Shrink on a Ward

Life is like a roller-coaster. It has its ups and downs.
But it's your choice to scream or enjoy the ride.

—F.W. PEABODY

I dreamt that I planned a center for Shamanistic studies. People would come from all over, but the center was in a remote place. Healing was done by creating: art, painting, writing, and chanting.

This dream was synchronistic as I incorporate active imagination in my own healing and in-depth therapy.[1] My view is like Jung's: that illness is creative.

I was quite depressed being away from Debbie and coped with this in my own shamanistic way by writing, painting, and being an analytic patient.[2]

As a staff-psychiatrist in 1976 and 1977, I worked in two in-patient units, each for six months. One was a ward for acutely and psychotically ill patients. The other was the Youth Drug Ward.

1. Rosen, D.H. (2002). *Transforming Depression: Healing the Soul through Creativity.* York Beach, ME: Nicolas-Hays.

2. Lommel, A. (1967). *Shamanism: The Beginnings of Art.* New York: McGraw Hill. See also Rosen, D.H. (1977). "The pursuit of one's own healing." *American Journal of Psychoanalysis* 37: 37–41.

Both were very stressful, but incredibly important for my own development. One of my patients, a young successful lawyer from the acute ward, was unable to drive across the Golden Gate Bridge because he knew he would stop and jump to his death. This was most likely due to the fact that he had an unconscious impulse to kill his parents, which was turned back on himself. Rather than cross the bridge, he would have to drive around the bay in order to get to Marin. This was very upsetting to him and his law firm. The goal of therapy was for him to be able to drive his car across the bridge without stopping and wanting to jump. Eventually, after developing insight into his neurosis, he was able to do this.

Another patient, an elderly woman, almost died from walking in front of a semi-truck. The truck stopped inches from her and she was hospitalized on my ward. She was suicidal because she had advanced ovarian cancer. After intensive treatment, she saw me as an out-patient. The critical and creative, life-saving transformative experience for this woman involved saving harp seals. She joined an organization led by Brian Davies and became a major advocate for saving these endangered animals.[3] I remember when her oncologist called to inform me that her metastatic cancer went away. He was mystified by this and stated, "It must have been spontaneous regression." However, I thought it was the metamorphosis of her self-destructive urge to one of self-acceptance and transformation.

When I was on the Youth Drug Ward, I resolved a lot of my "father-complex." The director of that ward, Fari Amini, was a Freudian analyst who was stern but kind. He was a whiz at math, just like my father. He reached out to me and we became good colleagues. Having been recently married, and grieving my father's death, he became an important figure for me.[4] When I was 28, my

3. Davies, B. (1989). *Red Ice: My Fight to Save the Seals*. London: Methuen London Ltd.

4. Rosen, D.H. (2014). *Lost in the Long White Cloud: Finding my Way Home*. Eugene, OR: Wipf & Stock.

dad died suddenly in a head on car collision. I have also always found Leonard Cohen to be an important and encouraging father figure. His music always soothed my mind, and actually he also rather looked like my father. Like so many others who feel broken or in need of encouragement, I find Cohen's words inspiring, "Ring the bells that still can ring, forget your perfect offering. There's a crack in everything, that's how the light gets in."

Leonard Cohen

made it look

easy.

I continued to lead a group therapy program that I started in 1975 with Chris Asimos to help serious suicide attempters. We had written about this earlier as a chapter in a book with other colleagues who were involved in the same activity.[5] This group therapy program was successful, as none of the members ended up committing suicide. Because of Chris's Greek background and my own love of that country, we frequented Greek restaurants and after eating, we danced through the suicidal problems. This underscores the value of dance as a form of in-depth therapy.[6]

5. Rosen, D.H., Asimos, C., Motto, J.A., & Billings, J.H. (1975). "Group psychotherapy with a homogenous group of suicidal persons." In A. Uchtenhagen, R. Battegay, and A. Friedemann (Eds.), *Group Therapy and Social Environment*. Ber: Verlag, Hans Huber, pp.201–212.

6. Chodorow, J. (1991). *Dance Therapy and Depth Psychology: The Moving Imagination*. New York: Routledge.

Chapter 4: Teaching Medicine

Our beliefs are really rules for action. To develop a thought's meaning,
we need only determine what conduct it is fitted to produce; that
conduct is for us its sole significance.

—WILLIAM JAMES[1]

*I dreamt that Freud had sexual problems. He used to hide under
water and use reeds to breathe and would watch women swim and
fish reproduce.*

Freud wrote that it was hard to work with female patients, but
it helped him master his conflicts. But the dream has to do with
myself, as I was a new father to my first-born daughter and dreaming of embracing my anima and being an analyst. In my practice,
I found that I had the opposite view from Freud, and preferred to
deal with women. It might have come from the same inner con-
flict—frustration with my anima—but we took different paths to
deal with this.

During this time, I saw a Freudian analyst, Dr. Fred Alston
as I had to deal with my own depression and authoritarian issues.

1. James, William. *The Writings of William James: A Comprehensive Edition.* Ed. John J. McDermott. New York: Random House, 1967. (p.377)

The rug, couch, and curtains were all a dark blue velvet color. In an odd way, this reflected the analyst's depression, as well as my own.

After I recovered from my despair, I switched to a Jungian, Dr. John Perry. I had always been drawn to Jung, who seemed maternal, more worldly, and holistic. Plus, Jung was an artist and a physician-scientist, like myself. His psychology encompasses the collective as well as the personal unconscious. Jung's non-reductive approach offered an expansive view of the psyche and world.

In the Spring of 1978, Deborah and I returned to the Shetland Islands to do a three year follow up of the subjects we interviewed originally. The project would only take place in the summer as the weather was more forgiving. In order to carry out this phase of the research, we hired a team of six interviewers who were graduate students in various fields from both the US and the UK. This expedited the interview process. We went to Christ's College in Cambridge in August to deliver a paper on our research at a NATO conference. This long-term project led to a subsequent publication that outlines what was found in this eco-psychological-medical study.[2]

In Shetland I had seen a chess set in the local museum which was carved by John Williamson of the Lubba (Ollaberry). He told me that it took him ten years to slowly carve the pieces in response to an ad in *The Shetland Times* calling for native crafts. I asked if he could carve another. He said, "No. It's too tedious for me." Then I asked if it would be possible to get casts made of his pieces to make a replica. He couldn't believe that I would want to do such a thing, but he agreed to it.

---

2. Voorhees-Rosen, D.J. & Rosen, D.H. (1981). "Shetland: The effects of rapid social change on mental health." In: S.A. Mednick and A.E. Baert (Eds.), *Prospective Longitudinal Research: An Empirical Basis for the Primary Prevention of Psychosocial Disorders.* Oxford: Oxford University Press, 178–188.

Replica of the Chess Set

In August, Debbie and I travelled to Honolulu, Hawaii with our one year old daughter, Sarah. We presented our Shetland Health Study research at the World Congress of Psychiatry.[3]

Young bamboo
no worries

Later that year, a successful grant proposal with Dr. Wallerstein, titled "The Psychiatric Aspects of Medical Practice," was funded by the Henry J. Kaiser Family Foundation. This project, funded from 1978–1982, was a clinical education program at every teaching hospital in the UCSF clerkship system. It involved sixty faculty members and was taught every week in two hour blocks. The medical students presented their patients on their clinical clerkships, which involved medicine, surgery, neurology,

3. Rosen, D.H. and Voorhees-Rosen, D.J. "Shetland: The effects of rapid social change on mental health" in Honolulu, Hawaii, at the World Congress of Psychiatry, August 31, 1977.

pediatrics, obstetrics-gynecology, and ambulatory community medicine.[4]

Around this time, I decided to pursue training in Jungian psychoanalysis. I applied and was accepted as a candidate in the C.G. Jung Institute in San Francisco. Once there, I met and and got to know Joe Wheelwright. Though an analyst, Joe was a very happy person and a great analyst. I really looked to him as a mentor, and tried to overcome my own depression and take on a happier, healthier disposition. Also, Joe had met Jung in Switzerland, so I was lucky enough to hear a number of stories about Jung over the whisky we would sometimes sneak in his office when relaxing after sessions. Both Joe and his wife Jane were analysts, and they are both featured in the documentary film, *Matter of Heart*.

Who knows why one chooses the path they do. I suppose Jungian psychology had always seemed more relevant to life and its activities. I didn't know it at the time, but my bourgeoning interest in Jung and the collective unconscious would be one of the most influential and meaningful aspects of my life. Not only would my work with Jung support my own self actualization, by affirming my artistic and personal growth, it would also introduce me to an incredible and growing community of scholars, friends, and analysts that continue to impact and be important to me to this day.

4. Rosen, D.H. and Blackwell, B.L. (1977) "Teaching the psychiatric aspects of medicine: Report of a successful pilot experience" in *Proceedings of the Sixteenth Annual Conference on Research in Medical Education*. Washington, D.C.: Association of American Medical Colleges. See also Rosen, D.H. and Blackwell, B. (1982). "Teaching psychiatry in medicine: The development of a unique clinical course." *Archives of Internal Medicine* 142, 1113–1116.

Chapter 5: The Berkeley Years

Life is about creating yourself.

—GEORGE BERNARD SHAW

I dreamt that I was at a religious convention and turned into my colleague, Jerry Motto, who was Jewish and a suicidologist like myself.

A spiritual creative part my journey was looking after my inner self. I was actualizing the concept of egocide and transformation. I was in a transition period of being a caring doctor and a physician-scientist. Dr. Motto was also a researcher in the area of suicide. Once at San Francisco General Hospital, I remember how kind and competent he was with a female intern-colleague, who wanted to kill herself because her husband was in Vietnam. I walked her to Dr. Motto's office and he gave her hope.

In 1979, after concluding our research in Shetland, Debbie and I returned to our hillside home in Berkeley, California. The grant and the courses I was teaching led to a national conference on medical education and the psychosocial and psychiatric aspects of medical practice, which I hosted at UCSF. It featured two keynote speakers. The first, Norman Cousins, gave a talk on "The physician as humanist." His presentation was later published as a foreword to *Medicine as a Human Experience*.[1] Cousins was well-known for his important popular book, *Anatomy of an Illness*, which discusses his experience of curing his severe and potentially fatal illness through laughter.[2] Cousins decided to leave the hospital with his doctor's permission and check into a five-star hotel where he could have good food and watch Marx brothers movies. He also received large doses of vitamin C. As an aside, it may seem rather tragic that it is only with an enormous amount of money that one can heal themselves by not working and staying in luxurious five star hotels. Not everyone could afford that. But really, part of what makes this story interesting is that, with the amount of money American hospitals and insurance companies charge for "medicine" anyway, frankly, one could simply go to hotel and order five star food. Maybe, if people actually just had access to that kind of luxury and leisure, things would be better. At any rate, the second speaker, George Engel, spoke on "The psychosocial aspects of medicine." He was the originator of the biopsychosocial model in medicine.[3]

End to end sky

why despair

glimpse of heaven

In 1980, I was pleased when Engel invited me to come to The University of Rochester Medical Center to spend the summer as part of a NEH (National Endowment of Humanities) sponsored seminar on healing. Dr. Engel opened the meeting with

---

1. Reiser, D.E., and Rosen, D.H. (1984). *Medicine as a Human Experience*. Baltimore: University Park Press. See also Rosen, D.H. and Hoang, U.B. (2017). *Patient-Centered Medicine: A Human Experience*. New York: Oxford University Press. This updated edition also includes a foreword by Andrew Weil, MD.

2. Cousins, N. (2005). *Anatomy of an Illness: As Perceived by the Patient*. New York: W.W. Norton & Company.

3. Engel GL. The need for a new medical model: a challenge for biomedicine. Science. 196 (4286) 1977:129–36.

introductory remarks about how every psychological problem has a physical and cultural manifestation and that every physical problem has psychological and sociological aspects. This correlates were insights from his book, *Psychological Development in Health and Disease.*[4]

I was impressed by the multiple testimonies about how attitude, art, and even prayer were associated with healing. For example, a plastic surgeon talked about how he would pause and say a prayer outside a patient's room and imagine that the disfigured human face was like a gnarled tree that he would see in a forest. This helped him because he thought of the person as no different than a tree in need of care and restoration.

After the seminar, I was a member of a task force for the American Psychiatric Association. Together we wrote on how the environment affects emotional and psychological problems.[5] I continued giving talks on how to integrate the psychosocial factors in healing into medical education and practice.

In 1981, my wife gave birth to our second daughter, lovely Laura at Alta Bates Hospital in Berkeley. Having another baby while getting her PhD in psychology was a lot for her, and I was also busy with teaching, research, patients, training to become an analyst, and heading a consultation-liaison service at UCSF. But Laura was a very good, pleasant, and happy baby. She had the loveliest disposition, and she really added a wonderful dimension to our lives. Still, looking back, I recognize that, as two academics (one PhD candidate and one analyst in training) my wife and I were not ideal parents: academia, and especially the PhD process, demands everything from you and then some. I realize, now, that

---

4. Engel, G.L. (1962). *Psychological Development in Health and Disease.* Philadelphia and London: W.B. Saunders Company.

5. Shurley, J.T., Rosen, D.H., Chen, R., Norman, E.C., Esser, A.H., & Sengel, R.A. (1979). *Relating Environment to Mental Health and Illness.* Task Force Report 16, American Psychiatric Association. Washington, DC.

our being over-worked and under-slept, and having so many other commitments was not idea, and prevented us from being able to be there for our kids like we would have wanted to be. And, for my part, I regret any negative effect my own career has had on my growing kids, especially at such young ages. Still, Laura continued to grow into a lovely and kind young woman, and has always maintained the good nature she had, even as an infant.

Laura in 2014

Red dragonfly
what do you listen for
so deeply?

In 1982, I published a significant paper with Barbara Black-well, who was a researcher in the office of medical education at UCSF.[6] This article linked psychosocial and psychiatric aspects

6. Rosen, D.H. & Blackwell, B. (1982). "Teaching psychiatry in medicine:

of medicine with a patient's illness. For example, one professional woman of 30 with terminal cancer had recently gone through a difficult divorce. She wanted to live long enough to make sure her mother got possession of her daughter when she passed rather than her ex-husband. We presented her case and I got involved. A social worker helped make her wish come true. One day a medical student asked this woman if she was afraid of dying. She looked right in his eyes and said, "No. God likes young, accomplished, and beautiful people in heaven."

The development of a unique clinical course." *Archives of Internal Medicine* 142: 1113–1116.

Chapter 6: The Rochester Years

Certain is it that there is no kind of affection so purely angelic
as of a father to a daughter.

—JOSEPH ADDISON

*I dreamt I was sticking with Jungian analysis and going to end up
working as a Jungian analyst. I kissed a depressed woman in my
cohort at the Jung Institute in San Francisco. Then I had a realization: I am it, it is me.*

I wanted to finish my Jungian training. Hence, I'm embracing my
depressed anima. I kissed her to bring that part of me to life.

Also, at this time, the dream was sort of facilitating our reloca-
tion to Rochester, where I had been asked but declined to take a
position at the University of Rochester. This dream made me feel
confident that I would finish my degree, and that taking this position in Rochester would help me do so. So, in 1982, when Dr.
Engel formally invited me, I took him up on his invitation to work
alongside him. He facilitated and supported my receiving a position as a tenured professor in Psychiatry and Medicine.

But before the move, I took the opportunity to see Kay Brad-
way, a Jungian analyst and expert in sand tray therapy. She was
accepting and understanding of my feeling that I was ill and dying

from a terminal suicidal depression. But she thought my sand tray indicated death and rebirth, from being lost to finding my way. She said it's important to accept myself through the painful process of contacting and loving my depressed anima. In the sand tray I am that dark figure, the depressed spiritual being. I support an inner authority and am letting go of my negative father, the Freudian analyst, and my own father. Kay also felt my sand tray was not that of a morbid dying person because of the egg in the center, a baby, and an ancient fertile male symbol carrying a baby. She pointed out that the turtle, which is my talisman, indicated my slow, steady journey toward health. Kay listened and said I should rest and see a doctor if I wasn't better in a few days. I got extra sleep and recuperated on my own.

Sand tray therapy

Turtle
moves so slowly
wins the race

In the summer of 1982, we finally moved to Rochester. I was in charge of the Consultation/Liaison Service which involved being called to every unit in the hospital. I was well-prepared for this work as I had been in charge of the same division at UCSF. Fortunately, Debbie was able to do her internship at the same institution.

I worked closely with Dr. Engel. Utilizing his biopsychosocial model in clinical practice, I headed the service that he started, which incorporated nursing, social work, and psychology in his rounds with a patient. For instance, Dr. Engel always started his rounds in the emergency room and followed the patient to the medical or surgical floor. It was very unusual for a doctor to incorporate all these different aspects of clinical history and care, and I found them very compelling and interesting practices. I kept up this practice when I received Engel's position. However, I added a spiritual dimension by having the chaplain attend our rounds. The chaplain would introduce us to patients in need of spiritual counseling. For example, there was a middle aged man with melanoma who was married with two kids, and he was concerned about burdening his wife and children. Hospice was suggested and called in to address all of the physical, social, mental, and spiritual needs of the patient.

In 1983, we expanded our Shetland study to consider the drinking problem among Shetlanders, who had an extremely high rate of alcoholism.[1] We started working with Raul Caetano and Richard Suzman on the problems related to alcohol consumption.

Our third daughter, Rachel, was born in Strong Memorial Hospital at the University of Rochester Medical Center on April 20, 1984. Rachel was a lively and energetic baby, and she was sort of a star in our young family, adding a lightness and brightness.

1. Caetano, R., Suzman, R.M., Rosen, D.H., & Voorhees-Rosen, D.J. (1982). The Shetland Islands: Drinking patterns in the community. *British Journal of Addiction* 77: 415–429; Caetano, R., Suzman, R.M., Rosen, D.H., & Voorhees-Rosen, D.J. (1983). The Shetland Islands: Longitudinal changes in alcohol consumption in a changing environment. *British Journal of Addiction* 78: 21–36.

This is an aspect of her personality which she has maintained. Having young children took me back to being a young child, and I strived to be a more present parent to my own daughters. Inspired by Rachel's birth and working through my own issues, I wrote my first children's book, *Henry's Tower*, which is a story about a young boy's struggle to understand and cope with an emotionally disturbed father.[2] This book was used in bibliotherapy with children of mentally ill veterans.

Rachel in 2017

2. Rosen, D.H. (1984). *Henry's Tower*. Pittsford, NY: Platypus Books.

Gentle rain...

star magnolia

glistens

I would often go to Toronto, Canada to see Marion Woodman and Daryl Sharp for control analysis (supervision) as part of my analytic training.

In 1984, I co-authored *Medicine as a Human Experience* with David Reiser.[3] To our amazement, this book was featured in *The New York Times*. During this year, I published multiple articles in *The New Physician* and *Journal of the American Medical Association*.

Cover of Medicine as a Human Experience

3. Reiser, D.E. and D.H. Rosen. (1985). *Medicine as a Human Experience.* Gaithersburg, MD: Aspen Publishers. (Originally published in 1984 by University Park Press). An updated and expanded version of this book was written with Uyen Hoang. See Rosen, D.H. and U. Hoang. (2017). *Patient-Centered Medicine: A Human Experience.* New York: Oxford University Press.

After Christmas, I went on a week-long retreat at a nearby Catholic, Trappist monastery called "The Abbey of the Genesee" in Piffard, New York. I stayed in the Bethlehem Retreat House and welcomed the solitude, silence, spiritual reading, and prayer. I went on the retreat to revise a paper on egocide and self-healing.[4] While there, I read Thomas Merton's *The Power and Meaning of Love.*[5] The abbot father, John Eudes Bamburger, told me that Merton was his teacher at the Abbey of Our Lady of Gesthemene. Bamburger joined a monastery after completing his psychiatry residency. One of Bamburger's tasks in the Catholic world was interviewing potential monks regarding their emotional health. This impressed me as he was a thoughtful, kind, and introspective person.

During the retreat, I wrote in my journal, "Today is the beginning of the rest of my life." At Vespers, I chanted psalms with the monks and told myself repeatedly, "God help me, I surrender. Guide me, my soul is in your hands." I experienced a spiritual transformation in which death and life were the same.

In a dream, I kept hearing "the work must go on." Then I was back in a hospital similar to where I did my internship, getting a book from a colleague that was on philosophy by Henri Bergson called Creative Evolution.

This dream emphasized my continued work in academic and the importance of writing books and incorporating creative things into my work and life. Like Bergson, I had many creative impulses and his book turned out to be very influential.[6]

---

4. Rosen, D.H. (1989). "Modern Medicine and the Nature of the Healing Process. *Humane Medicine: A Journal of the Art and Science of Medicine* 5: 18–23.

5. Merton, T. (2010). *The Power and Meaning of Love.* London: SPCK Publishing.

6. Bergson, H. (1998). *Creative Evolution.* New York: Dover Publications.

Chapter 7: Texas is a State of Mind

Where danger is there rises the saving one also.

FRIEDRICH HÖLDERLIN

I dreamt that I witnessed young medical students getting awards—the best at this and that award. I thought, "I'm older and beyond that."

Even at the time, I was not "beyond that," but was very wrapped up in the awards and recognition. To this day I still reflect on all that this dream is working through: my struggle with recognition. I have always felt insecure and wanted to receive awards to demonstrate my success and make me feel proud. But at the same time, I have always known that awards and recognition boast no long-term fulfillment. They are not the meaningful things in life, and yet academia especially teaches us that that's what makes us important. Most of my career has been teaching medical students and others, and I have been recognized for my work. But I now know that awards are not the be all and end all of everything— instead teaching and helping other students is what is rewarding.

In August 1986, I went to a family camp under the pressure of Debbie to spend time with our friends, Tony and Lynne, and their two children. To be honest, I didn't like family camp. I'm an introvert and I don't like being around a lot of people and being herded into doing activities. However, I liked the setting, which was peaceful and beautiful. I enjoyed swimming there and being with my children.

Family Camp

A month later, I was traveling first class (a rare occasion for me, but I had the miles to do so) on an airplane from New York to Texas. I sat next to a tall cowboy. I was so enamored that I watched his every move. At first he took the cowboy hat off his head and put it carefully in the overhead bin. After we ascended, the flight attendant came by and asked what we would like to drink. He ordered a whiskey neat and I had a gin and tonic.

Then he asked me in a Southern drawl, "Where are you goin' and why?" "I'm going to a job interview at Texas A&M." He suddenly changed his demeanor and became very friendly. I turned and said, "You would know the answer to this question. What kind of state is Texas? Is it Southern, Southwestern, or Midwestern?" He took another sip, leaned back, and responded, "It's not none of those." "Well, what is it then?" He paused for a while. Then he looked in my eyes and very slowly said, "Texas....is a state of mind." After another pause, he continued, "I'm so excited that you're goin' to Texas A&M. That's where I went. It's the best university in the world. No question about it. It's the public Harvard of Texas."

Chapter 7: Texas is a State of Mind

I was interviewing for a unique position, the McMillan Professorship in Analytical Psychology. I recall asking Dr. Engel about such a position. He said that I should take it if I was selected because an endowed professorship was prestigious and came with funding for research. The idea of not writing grants and running a service was very appealing. I also thought that it would allow me to spend more time with my children.

The interview went surprisingly well. At first glance, Texas A&M looks like a military installation or a prison. However, the people were extremely friendly, competent, and kind. This baffled me and Debbie because it broke down our prejudice of Texas being a backward state. It was an important lesson—like Heraclitus believed, everything goes to the opposite.

Two weeks later, I got a call from the Department Head offering me the position. He even threw in a lectureship for Debbie to get us to come. They brought both of us back to Texas so we could start looking for a house. Our realtor found a Guggenheim house. It was large, beautiful, and had a swimming pool, as well as a hot tub. The family that had been there also had three girls. The house was very simpatico with our needs and beyond our expectations. We quickly put down an offer and it was accepted. It was to our benefit that, just as we bought the house, the economy was at a downturn, so we got a fantastic house for quite a steal.

My three daughters, around the time we moved.

It's wonderful when synchronicity happens. We had flown to Dallas and then Mr. Guggenheim flew us down to College Station in his private jet. This show of generosity and kindness impressed us greatly. I decided to accept the position for the growth of myself and my family.

Bloom in the desert. . .
be myself in America's outback!

The sun shines bright
Things seem right
Jung in the soul of Texas!

Dr. Engel's parting gift

But all was not right in the world. Despite the Guggenheim, Debbie wanted to stay in Rochester. I felt so alone as she became negative and distant. But I felt this was the right move for us and our family. Eventually she came around and accepted the adventure of going to Texas. The impending move was very stressful. I was depressed, but still hopeful about it. I believed I was blessed with my family and work.

At that time, I was seeing Paul Kugler, a Jungian analyst, in Buffalo, New York. He was a bright, sensitive, and kind person. Working with him helped me to deal with inner and outer conflictual issues. When leaving, in my last session, I told Paul that we don't need to cry because I would see him in Jungian analytic circles later.

Before we left, I visited my childless godparents, Sam and Claire Silverman. Sam, a New York State Supreme Court Judge, had sent me a picture of himself and Bobby Kennedy during Kennedy's campaign. My mother liked both of them as they had a mixed marriage just like my parents. She was Catholic and Sam was a childhood friend of my father's. When I was little, I used to think that I wouldn't mind living with them if anything happened to my parents. Sam was would tell me about how smart, talented, and artistic my dad was. It was fun being around Sam and Claire, as they loved life. When I visited, they would take me to lovely restaurants and Broadway plays. Sam had come to my father's funeral and burial, and in many ways became a surrogate father figure.

Chapter 8: Rebirth in the Friendly State

You may all go to Hell, and I will go to Texas.

—DAVY CROCKETT

I dreamt of my father who cut his left hand between the thumb and forefingers with a small axe. Why did father do that? I comforted him. He put a large bandaid on it, as it was not severe. Then we shook hands—my right, his left.

This speaks to the possibility of hurting myself as an authority figure. The fact that I comforted this part of myself is important as I was approving of my new job and the move.

Echoing this was a visit to the McMillan's in Corpus Christi, in which I experienced a closeness with Frank McMillan, Jr., who had endowed the position that I had accepted. I found it odd that a Texas oil man would fund the world's first professorship in Analytical Psychology. I asked him, "Why did you do such a thing?" He responded, "It's very simple. Jung saved my life." I asked if he had had Jungian analysis. He said, "No." "Well how did this come about?" He answered, "I helped myself by reading all the old man's Collected Works." I couldn't believe it. He said, "You gotta bring the lightening spirit of Jung into the darkness of these Aggies. They need help!" The McMillans became a second family. In fact, I'm still close to his son, Frank McMillan, III, who is like a brother.

Frank McMillan, IV, the son of Frank McMillan, III, shares the same godfather as Prince William: Sir Laurens van der Post. As a side story, once when I was in London, I met with Sir Laurens at his apartment. Over a cup of tea, we discussed an important dream that Frank McMillan, Jr. had had when he was six years old. Once at the Jung Center in Houston, he had asked Sir Laurens what the following dream meant. He dreamt that a lion came into his bedroom. He bolted up in his bed, scared to death. Then the lion came up to him and licked his cheek. Being from South Africa, Sir Laurens said to McMillan that this was a very special and telling dream. He looked at Frank and said, "You have a special mission in your life."

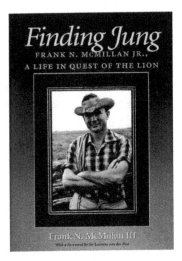

Frank McMillan, Jr.

The endowed position allowed me to develop two new courses: The Psychology of Self and The Psychology of Religion.[1]

1. See Rosen, D.H. (1994). "In Memoriam: Frank N. McMillan and the Circle of Friends of Analytical Psychology at Texas A&M University." *Journal of Analytical Psychology* 39: 121–127. McMillan III, F.N. and D.H. Rosen (2012). "Synchronicity at the Crossroads: Frank McMillan Jr., Forrest Bess, and Carl Jung." *Jung Journal: Culture & Psyche* 6(2): 86–102. McMillan III, F.N. (2012). *Finding Jung: Frank McMillan Jr., A Life in Quest of the Lion.* College Station, TX: Texas A&M.

I had always been interested in these topics so it was a pleasure and a gift to teach them. It also allowed me to teach both graduate and undergraduate students in these courses and work with future Ph.D. candidates.

In academia, one has to metaphorically juggle many things. I never took actual juggling lessons, but I wish I had. Maybe that would have helped. As the reader can imagine, it's a difficult task to juggle family, with a new house and three children, see psychiatric and analytic patients, and work full time as an academic with the pressures of writing, giving lectures, guest presentations, publications, and grants. In addition, my being in training to become a Jungian psychoanalyst was not valued by the faculty in my department. Jung was not valued at that time as an academic psychologist. Ironically, Freud was more valued, which fits with the patriarchal nature of psychology and its cognitive-behavioral nature. I remember at a department picnic, a behavioral psychologist came up to me and said, "Jung was not a behaviorist." I replied, "Yes he was." The dumbfounded professor asked, "What are you talking about?" I said, "Every dream, creative activity, and artistic production is grounded in behavior."[2] Later he held up a frisbee and said "Mandala." I responded, "You got it!"

I loved being a father with the kids swimming in the pool and helping them with projects. While Sarah knew how to swim, I would take Laura and Rachel to their swim lessons so we wouldn't have to worry about them in our pool. I had a nightly practice of taking walks with Rachel, my youngest daughter. I used to go to a nearby park with her and she loved to swing, swing, swing. She would say, "More daddy. Swing me high to the sky." I enjoyed reading to my daughters and tucking them into bed with love, hugs, and kisses. For example, I would read "The Butter Battle Book" by

---

2. Henderson, P.G., Rosen, D.H., & Mascaro, N. (2007). "Empirical study on the healing nature of mandalas." *Psychology of Aesthetics, Creativity, and the Arts* 1: 148–154.

Dr. Seuss to Laura.[3] And to twelve year old Sarah, I would read "A Pocket Full of Seeds" by Marilyn Sachs.[4]

Spring oaks. . .
serenity
sparkling

On July 4th, we all went to see fireworks at a community site.

As an intern in California, I had bought a new Karmann Ghia convertible, which I drove to Texas. It was a fun car because it was a joy to ride while being exposed to the elements. Unfortunately, I sold it in 1987 for the same price as I paid for it. I say it's unfortunate because now the car is a collector's item, as the body was designed by Porsche.

At this point in my life I was devoted to Jung's psychology, since that was the nature of my job. I started a Jungian group called the Brazos Valley Jungian Society. In this study group, we initially read Frieda Fordham's book, *An Introduction to Jung's Psychology.*[5] This volume as well as a text by June Singer formed the basis of a new curriculum that I was developing at TAMU.[6] It was this year that I first taught "Introduction to Analytical Psychology." The initial offering was so popular that graduate students also requested to attend the class. I developed a graduate version of this course soon thereafter. In addition, I began to accept PhD students to work with me.

Being a Jungian analyst and a physician in a traditional psychology department was difficult, to say the least. First of all, there

3. Seuss, D. (1984). *The Butter Battle Book.* New York: Random House.

4. Sachs, M. (2005). *A Pocket Full of Seeds.* Lincoln, NE: iUniverse Press.

5. Fordham, F. (1953). *An Introduction to Jung's Psychology.* New York: Penguin.

6. Singer, J. (1994). *Boundaries of the Soul: The Practice of Jung's Psychology.* New York: Anchor Books.

were no other physicians in the department, as most psychologists at the time were trained in psychology departments, not medical schools. Second, I learned quickly that in psychology at that time, Jung was *persona non grata*. It's not by accident that I was also reading "Of Human Bondage" by W. Somerset Maugham. It was during this period that I also felt an intense bond with William James. He was also a physician, and the first to teach a psychology course in the U.S. He was widely respected and the author of the first psychology text book. In fact, I had a fantasy that I could see his ghost walking down the dark halls of our psychology department.

I didn't let myself get down by colleagues that didn't value and respect me. Instead, I saw myself as a pioneer who was now able to actualize something I dreamed of. It was like the reverse of the Myth of Sisyphus. I was there because I loved my work only to have the Psychology department attempt to push it back down. However, it was helpful to have a dual appointment in Medicine, where I was a professor in Psychiatry and Humanities in Medicine, since my work was appreciated there.

Typical of my having a strong muse (anima or soul), I dreamt of a woman around 40 who looked like a natural goddess. The feminine energy I was feeling from this dream inspired me to be bold and creative, and to write on my own experience as a casualty of the health care system. In the dream, my anima was healthy and strong, and this helped me give birth to a project I had been wanting to write for a while, about all those who are not healthy and strong and who are wronged by our healthcare system (which I had seen so much of). I wrote a paper for the *Alpha Omega Alpha* Honor Medical Society's journal on the casualties of the health care system.[7] Parenthetically, I was honored to have been selected to be a member of *Alpha Omega Alpha* while in medical school, which is the medical equivalent of Phi Beta Kappa.

7. Rosen, D.H. (1987). "Casualties of the health care system: Patients depressed by medicine's 'moral dilemmas.'" *The Pharos* 50: 1920.

At this time I was meeting with the head of psychology at Texas A&M, Steve Worchel. When I went to his office, he was having a heated discussion with a female faculty member about why one spouse should not have an affair. I wondered why he was talking about that. The faculty member said she was against that happening. Soon thereafter she left the department for a job at a distant university. I tucked this away and later learned that he had even harassed my wife at the time.

Steve wanted me to use my endowment as part of my salary. I said no because that's not what the endowment was for. It was made to be used for my own research, graduate students, and to present at academic conferences. Fortunately, he was eventually forced out of the department.

It was a premonition when my family and I went to see Benji the Hunted, an excellent Disney movie about a lost dog who adopts a litter of mountain lion cubs. The movie had great nature photography of the Oregon coastal mountains and the animals of this region. Ironically, I would end up living in that same area (with a dog who looks just like Benji, as you'll see in the afterword).

My father and Mother

I continued my own analytic work with James (Jim) Aylward. I was dealing with dreams about two maverick shadow figures. They represented my father and a mythic Father, Chronos (Time), who killed his sons. This relates to the fact that my father envied me in that he always wanted to be a professor and scholar. He actually once was a lecturer in Zoology at Brooklyn College in NYC. With his patients, he embodied what doctor means in Greek, that is, "teacher." As an Eye, Ear, Nose, and Throat specialist, he always counseled his patients to prevent illnesses. In an act of altruism, he worked at the Federal Medical Prison in Springfield, Missouri. One day, he came home and asked if I had ever heard of a Rock-N-Roll singer named Chuck Berry who was one of his patients. He said that this man was in there for transporting a white girl across state lines. I told him that he was a famous singer and guitar player. My father characterized him as one of the nicest individuals that he'd ever met. While in prison there, Berry wrote two songs, "Nadine" and "No Particular Place to Go."

My mother was a poet in her own right. For instance, she published a book of poetry, *The Thin Mask*, with Crown Publishers in 1939. Although she married my father for love in 1938, and they were clearly happy in the early years of their marriage, by the mid 1940s, my father was a shellshocked casualty of the Pacific front of World War II. After that, my parents argued and seemed unhappy. My mother divorced my father, twice, and it caused my father to be very sad. Yet he never lost his love for her, as evidenced by the fact that they married a second time. I don't know for sure, but I have always thought that his death from a head on car collision shortly after the second divorce was possibly related to unconscious suicide.

Chapter 9: Adapting to a Cowboy Culture

He who wants a rose must respect the thorn.

—Persian Proverb

Settling into life in "Aggieland" was challenging. I was already well into the second year, which I called "The Ginger Year." The reason I called it "ginger" is that it's a rhizome that both burns and heals. It makes one lively and animated.

I felt like I was treading water. I was super busy: working in the clinic, seeing patients, carrying out research projects, supervising PhD students, and setting up new courses in the Psychology of Religion and Analytical Psychology (later called Psychology of Self). I taught undergraduates, graduate students, and medical students. With all students I focused on healing the whole person.[1]

At the time, I was working in the clinical division of psychology, and I recall presenting the case of a suicidal patient. This young man's parents divorced, the father was authoritarian and the mother was distant and non-nurturing. I had him draw his family, which helped to get them out of his head. Part of therapy was to get him to differentiate self from family. As I've found before with

---

1. Rosen, D.H. and U. Hoang. (2017). *Patient-Centered Medicine: A Human Experience*. New York: Oxford University Press.

seriously depressed patients, drawing helps and heals.[2] Following his artwork, a turning point was when he circled a square. This is symbolic of the feminine circling the masculine, so in a way he was rebirthing himself.

I dreamt just one word in neon lights: LOVE. I noted in my journal that love is the key to all relationships. During this time of my life, this was true of my relationship with Debbie. We were a loving family and everything at work and home seemed right.

However, I continued to suffer from horrible migraines, which had to do with juggling multiple tasks between my family and professional life. Plus, the Klu Klux Klan burned a cross in our lawn, which really upset me. This was a reaction to writing a letter in the local newspaper supporting anti-apartheid activities in South Africa. Debbie was helpful. She used to rub my neck to help me feel better, and I would call her a shaman.

On one of my trips to the Jung Educational Center in Houston, I met Carolyn Fay and her husband, Ernest. Carolyn was one of the founders of this educational center, which Frank McMillan frequented and gave money to. She was impressed by his generosity.

On another trip to the Jung Center, Carolyn and Ernest invited me to their lovely home. We sat on the veranda and Ernest served delicious mint juleps, which he proudly made himself. Sadly, he died in a sailboating accident shortly after that. This was ironic because he was a former Olympian in sailing.

Carolyn subsequently gave that house to one of her daughters to start a Fay School for young children. Carolyn then moved into a penthouse apartment overlooking Hermann Park in downtown Houston. When I visited her, she answered the doorbell personally, instead of hiring a butler or maid. She had invited me to have

2. Rosen, D.H. (2002). *Transforming Depression: Healing the Soul Through Creativity.* York Beach, ME: Nicolas-Hays.

lunch at her place. She opened the door and I saw a beautiful painting that was about three by five feet. I said, "Wow, what a beautiful painting. It looks like a Chagall." In her quiet, eloquent, and slow Texas drawl, she said, "Da-vid, that is a Cha-gall." I liked her a lot because she was so down to earth. I watched her put together our lunch by hand. This was important to me as it grounded her. We would often go out for lunches or early dinners together. Despite her determination to always pay for our meals, I got up the nerve to work out an arrangement with her that we would alternate. She reluctantly agreed.

I had the idea of establishing a lecture and book series in analytical psychology, but I needed funding for this. After meeting with the development office at TAMU, I was encouraged to ask Carolyn for $1,000,000. However, I was reluctant to do this because asking anyone for that kind of money was foreign to me. The development officer said, "You don't realize that asking her for that amount of money would be like asking me for a thousand dollars." I responded, "I'm sorry, I'm unable to do that. I'll ask her for $100,000 and no more." Carolyn agreed to fund the endowment, but she wanted it made in her late husband's name as well as her own.

I dreamt of riding a bull and planting new crops.

This dream was prophetic of an early patient I saw in College Station. The patient was a 21 year old student at Texas A&M, who was brought in by his mother. When I went to the waiting room to meet him, his mother started to come with him. I told her to please wait and that I wanted to talk with her son first. When we got in the office, he said that his mother thought he was mentally ill. All he wanted to do was to drop out of the university and ride bulls in the rodeo. I said, "Wow! That would be a difficult thing to do." He explained, "Yes, but that's what I love. Rodeo is my life." He seemed like an intelligent and sensitive young man, so I said, "Let me get your mother and have her come in." When they were both seated in the office, I looked at her and said, "Your son is not mentally imbalanced." She asked, "What do you mean?" I replied, "Rodeo-ing is not a mental illness. Your son seems like an intelligent and brave young man, and I wish him all the best in his career." She was aghast, so I offered my services to her, but she refused.

Reflecting on Texas A&M and what it means, the A is for agricul-ture (hence, the planting of new crops in the dream) and the M is for mechanics (engineering). However, I told myself that the A was for analysis and the M was for meditation. I even once put this in a professional article as a footnote as it was true to me.

In 1988, I worked on publishing medical cases from Rochester. One of these was a most unusual case of attempted suicide. The pa-tient had repeatedly injected himself intravenously with elemental mercury. Understandably, this patient turned out to be psychotic, so the healing process involved transferring him from a medical ward to a psychiatric unit.[3]

I also traveled to present at a number of conferences in 1988. In March, I presented a paper with two female PhD students in psy-chology at the National Conference of the Association for Women in Psychology at Bethesda, Maryland. Our essay explored the problem of depression in women from a Jungian point of view.[4] I traveled to Los Angeles in April to give a talk for a conference on "Youth Suicide: An In-Depth Perspective." The talk was on "Ego-cide and Transcendence: A Meaningful Alternative to Suicide," which was, and is, particularly applicable to teenagers.

I remember going to open houses for my daughters at their school. Once we got home, Sarah wanted me to quiz her on her spelling words and the state capitols. At age seven, Laura was able to read

3. Giombetti, R.J., Rosen, D.H., Kuczmierczyk, A.R., & Marsh, D.O. (1988). Repeated suicide attempts by the intravenous injection of elemental mercury. *The International Journal of Psychiatry in Medicine* 18: 153–167.

4. Rosen, D.H., Michas, E.A., & Hass, S.D. "Depression in Women: A Jungian Perspective." *National Conference of the Association for Women in Psy-chology.* Bethesda, MD, March 5, 1988.

whole books on her own. Rachel, who was four, still wanted to be read to. In the evenings, I would take Rachel on "moon-walks" and I remember saying, "Watch. . .Rachel, the moon is following us."

My analysis continued and I had dreams of my father, mother, and their ancestors. During this time, I was kinder to myself. I had fewer headaches, fears, depression, and self-deprecation.

I dreamt of a dark woman who was bruised on the face.

The following day, Debbie fell ill and had a terrible cough. I gave her my doctor's name. He said she had walking pneumonia. I was struck by the fact that she was claiming she wasn't ill. Because of her sickness, I took the kids out to eat and stayed up late reading *Jung and Feminism*, an excellent book by Demaris Wehr.[5]

Jim Aylward, my analyst, liked my first Texas painting that I brought to our therapy session. It was titled "Circle of Life" and utilized the four function colors of Jolande Jacobi.[6] Blue—depression; red—anger; yellow—happiness; green—growth; and orange, a mixture of yellow and red, is transformation.

"Circle of Life"

5. Wehr, D. (1987). *Jung and Feminism: Liberating archetypes.* New York: Routledge.

6. Jacobe, J. (2013). *Psychology of C G Jung.* New York: Routledge.

I made this note in my journal on September 11, 1988: Rosh Hashanah—The Jewish New Year—which calls for hope (ten days of charitable acts, then Yon Kippur, the day of atonement). I recall feeling optimistic about the future. I felt close with Debbie and our growing family.

Cold grey wind. . .

warming to gold

I dreamt of giving a lecture at the medical school on "Heal Thyself." This was prophetic because I ended up publishing articles and books related to this topic.

Another dream involved Jesse Jackson, who ran for president in 1988. I was attracted to his qualities of unification, courage, and spirit. This was unconsciously prophetic, as Barack Obama would become the first Black President of the United States in 2008.

At this time, another dream involved a positive interaction with Pat Berry (the wife of James Hillman at the time) who was involved in my training to become a Jungian analyst. When I woke up I had a good feeling, as becoming an analyst was an arduous, yet healing, process. It started in the Pacific Northwest, when I went to a meeting at the Jungian analytic training program of the Inter-Regional Society of Jungian Analysts (IRSJA), held at Mt. Hood. This was ironic, as I later would live and retire in Eugene, Oregon, not far from this mountain.

As I would do sometimes, twelve-year old Sarah and I made a special trip to Houston to see an extremely creative performance of Hansel and Gretel. Sarah and I had fun and we went out to eat afterwards and to shop. When we returned home later that night, Debbie was distant.

The day before Christmas I had a dream that I went to Armenia to help them rebuild after an earthquake. When I woke up, I thought

I had had a stroke because my left arm and leg were weak and tingling. Looking back, this may have been an unknown beginning of MS.

As this year ended, I dreamt that Steve Martin was with a cool and pragmatic brown-haired woman. I asked Martin if they were married and he said, "Why would I do that? I have everything I want." However, she looked pained, like she didn't want the relationship.

The dream was meaningful, as a successful marriage is based on an inner-marriage as Jung maintained. It involves loving your whole self. For example, a man would love his feminine side (or anima) and a woman would love her masculine side (or animus). When each individual loves him or herself, then you have a whole person, and two individuals can truly love each other.

Chapter 10: Medicine & Jung
in the Lone Star State

One cannot consent to creep when one has an impulse to soar.

—HELEN KELLER

Happy New Year! January 1, 1989. What a lovely day! I made swedish pancakes and fresh squeezed orange juice, grapefruit, and Pete's Coffee. Positive talk with Debbie. However, she's sick. She was awakened by an early call from her mother. She didn't tell her she was sick. I had the kids and took them to a friend's house. Lolly (Laura Torbet, whom my second daughter was named after), a dear friend, was visiting. She's a writer and painter. I asked her about writing a book together on suicide for a general readership. She wasn't interested. Five years later, after going to a writer's conference, I would write the book myself.[1]

On January 2nd, I dreamt I was doing too many things. This was true and made my life difficult.

For example, I gave an invited lecture at the Medical School for Harry Lipscomb's class, "Introduction to the Patient." The patient was a 53 year-old woman who had MS. Her illness developed in

1. Rosen, D.H. (1993). *Transforming Depression: A Jungian Approach Using the Creative Arts.* New York: Putnam.

the context of recent moves and her father's sudden death from leukemia. However, her husband was very supportive. Dr. Lipscomb sensitively referred her to a self-help group.

I was preparing a syllabus for Psychology of Religion, a course which I developed. I didn't realize at the time that the course was about myself and my search for purpose and spiritual meaning in life.

On my birthday, February 25th, I turned 44. Ironically, the candidates in the IRSJA were meeting in Memphis, where Elvis had lived. I thought of the death of poor Elvis, who actually died when he was about 40. When I visited Graceland, I wondered how someone so talented could have been so self-destructive. Going through his home on a tour gave me the heebie-jeebies. I felt odd going into someone's personal home. At the start of the tour, I noticed a Buddha sculpture sitting on the end-table by a couch. I thought, "How fascinating that he would be interested in Buddhism." A seed must have been planted in my mind to do a philosophical-psychological study of his life.[2]

In 1989, the year of the duck, I developed the duck response. It was necessary, as unfortunately, Jung was not well-regarded by the faculty in my department. The duck response involves either duck (get out of the way so you don't get hit) or let it run off like water from a duck's back (when it does get hit). This is ironic because I would later move to Eugene, which is the home of the Oregon Ducks.

When I taught the first class of Psychology of Religion, there were 40 students. I wore a shirt and kept my collar open with no tie. I said, "Welcome, this will be an open collar class." I explained, "We're going to be open to all religions of the world, which you will notice are very similar." Nearly every religion we discussed was represented by students in the class. I also invited practitioners

2. Rosen, D.H. (2002). *The Tao of Elvis*. Orlando: Harcourt.

of each religion to give guest presentations. For example, I had a white Christian male minister, a tall black Buddhist woman professor, a Catholic sister, and a totally average bearded Rabbi talk to the class. With the class mostly made up of white Southern Baptists, this was a shock to their system. When the Christian spoke, they seemed very comfortable. When the Buddhist spoke, they seemed edgy, but they watched and listened carefully, yet with suspicion. When the Catholic nun spoke, you could tell that some prejudice was apparent. They were very skeptical of her as she said she was married to Jesus and made rocking movements as she embraced the imaginary Savior in front of them. A female honor student came to see me in my office hours after the Rabbi spoke. She said, "Dr. Rosen, my family said that Jews are evil, but the Rabbi seemed like a kind human being." She didn't realize that my name and background was Jewish. I said, "You're right. He's no different than you and me."

In this class, I gave a lecture on one's personal spiritual experience. I talked about my own at the Trappist monastery, The Abbey of the Genesee, in Piffard, New York. I told the students about the death of my ego and the value of that transformation. I disclosed that I saw a woman on a snowy path in front of me. When she turned and faced me, I thought she looked like the Virgin Mary. When I shared this unusual experience with the abbott of the monastery, John Eudes Bamburger, he didn't act surprised. He said, "I have seen her too on the same path." During that retreat I had read important books on religious experience by Thomas Merton, Victor Frankl, Martin Buber, Carl Jung, and William James.[3]

Then there was an earthquake dream. It was scary, but I knew it was not the end.

3. Merton, T. (1999). *The Seven Storey Mountain*. New York: Mariner's Books;

Frankl, V. (1959). *Man's Search for Meaning*. Boston: Beacon Press; Buber, M. (1970). *I and Thou*. New York: Touchstone; Jung, C.G. (1933). *Modern Man In Search of a Soul*. New York: Houghton Mifflin Harcourt; James, W. (1902). *The Varieties of Religious Experience*. New York: Penguin.

I went to see my Jungian analyst, Jim Aylward, who was also a Catholic priest. I was drawn to him because he was once the director of the Jung Center in Houston and he gave mass to homeless individuals. He also had met Jung when he was in training in Switzerland.

In one of our sessions, he announced, "I can hear." I acted surprised. He said, "I just got hearing aids in both ears and I can actually hear you." I thought, "I was paying for analysis from someone who couldn't fully hear me?" Then I realized how important it was to *see* and accept the individual. I was also thankful that he could now hear me fully and clearly.

On March 15th of this year, Sarah became a teenager. I couldn't believe that we had a teen in the house. Anna Freud was once heard saying "adolescence is a normal psychosis." But, it was more than simply having a teenager. I also had a marriage that was on the edge, and Debbie and I were really struggling. We had difficulty co-parenting, since I did not agree with some of the things she was saying to our kids. In particular, I felt like she was trying to drive a wedge between myself and the kids, and painting me as a dark figure. This hurt me, and precipitated more marital therapy with a therapist named Betz.

Since I was a professor in both liberal arts and medicine, I focused on bridging these two fields in my life and scholarship. Healing always involves the biological, psychological, social, and cultural. This was the essence of modern medicine, which became the subject of a paper I wrote highlighting these issues.[4]

In 1990, Verena Kast turned in her book for the inaugural volume of the Carolyn and Ernest Fay book series in Analytical

4. Rosen, D.H. (1989). "Modern medicine and the nature of the healing process." *Humane Medicine: A Journal of the Art and Science of Medicine* 5: 18–23.

Psychology. This innovative pioneer was the first female president of the International Association for Analytical Psychology. Her book, *Joy, Inspiration, and Hope*, was based on the first lectures of this important series, which was established to further the ideas of C.G. Jung among students, faculty, therapists, and citizens.[5]

The Fay Book and Lecture Series addresses topics of importance to the individual and society. They were generously endowed by Carolyn Grant Fay, the founding president of the C.G. Jung Educational Center in Houston, Texas. Carolyn Fay planted a Jungian tree carrying both her name and that of her late husband, and has yielded fruitful ideas and stimulated creative works. As the McMillan Professor in Analytical Psychology, I was in charge of editing and writing the forewords for these original works.[6] This series grew to include twenty volumes. After I retired from Texas A&M in 2011, the endowment for these activities shifted to the Jung Educational Center.

I began 1990 by giving a lecture to the Houston A&M Mothers Club. The talk was titled, "Understanding Suicide with a Specific Focus on Preventing Youth Suicides." Meaningfully, it was held at a United Methodist Church. I imagine, but don't know, that this was precipitated by someone in the audience being familiar with a youth that committed suicide or was suicidal. I was glad to do this because I thought it was enlightened for this group to focus on such a critical issue. It also introduced me to the unique emphasis at Texas A&M on the family and spiritual connections.

Following this, on March 2nd, I gave an invited lecture presentation as part of an interdisciplinary literature conference, entitled, "The Fantastic Imagination in New Critical Theories," held at Texas A&M. My talk was on "Archetypes of Transformation: The Healing Aspects of Active Imagination in Literature, Film, and Art."

5. Kast, V. (1991). *Joy, Inspiration, Hope*. College Station, TX: Texas A&M University Press.

6. A full list of the books is available in appendix 1.

On April 20th, I was asked to give a TeleMedicine lecture for a Canadian audience on "Modern Medicine and the Nature of the Healing Process." TeleMedicine is an innovative technique that allows a doctor to talk to interested patients through a computer.

Following this, I traveled to Boston to give a presentation at the Annual Meeting of the American Psychological Association. It was on "Psychological Well-Being Among African American College Students." I co-authored the paper with Robin Nottingham, a PhD student at Texas A&M.

In the summer, I travelled to Antioch University in Yellow Springs, Ohio to attend a Writer's Workshop (because I had always secretly wanted to be a writer). If you've never been, Yellow Springs is lovely. It is a quaint little town, and at that time, there was a ton of milkweed in bloom. I was impressed by Joyce Carol Oates's keynote address. I had read her work and I was touched by her presence. She was a depressed, extremely sensitive, but down to earth and kind person. Her honesty affected me deeply. The whole experience was catalyst for me becoming a writer.

Showy milkweed. . .
keep smiling

That September, I presented a paper at Corpus Christi College at Oxford University. I was awestruck by the experience of being at Oxford. The talk was on "The Healing Archetype of the Doctor-Patient Relationship." It was an awe-inspiring and humbling experience to be a part of a conference on "The Archetype of the Healer." At this meeting, I was fortunate to meet and get to know Anthony Stevens, who would later be the third Fay lecturer, author, and alter a really dear, friend.[7]

7. Stevens, A. (1993). *The Two Million-Year-Old Self*. College Station, TX: Texas A&M University Press. Stevens, A. (2015). *Archetype Revisited*. New York: Routledge.

What good fortune to be able to travel and give such wide-ranging talks and presentations in so many places around the globe.

Chapter 11: Meaning in Melancholia

> You largely constructed your depression. It wasn't given to you.
> Therefore, you can deconstruct it.
>
> —ALBERT ELLIS

I dreamt of a young man dying of cancer.

More old shadow issues of my depressive illness.

In 1991, I travelled to historic New Harmony, Indiana to complete a book on depression.[1] I went at the invitation of Jane Blaffer Owen, who had restored the important early historic community of New Harmony.[2] I had met Jane through her interest in Jung, friendship with Carolyn Fay, and her attendance at the Fay Lectures in College Station. She not only provided time and space for me to write, she also gave me invaluable feedback and support. It's uncommon for people to respond so favorably to such a subject as depression, but she was encouraging.

---

1. Rosen, D.H. (2002). *Transforming Depression: Healing the Soul through Creativity.* York Beach, ME: Nicolas-Hays. First published by Putnam in 1993 and Viking/Penguin in 1996.

2. Owen, J.B. (2015). *New Harmony Indiana: Like a River, Not a Lake.* Bloomington: Indiana University Press.

Chapter 11: Meaning in Melancholia

The poet Rilke wrote in *Letters to a Young Poet* about the value of entering your depression: "Why do you want to shut out of your life any uneasiness, any misery, any depression, since after all you don't know what work these conditions are doing inside you? Why do you want to persecute yourself with the question of where all this is coming from and where it is going? Since you know, after all, that you are in the midst of transitions and you wished for nothing so much as to change. If there is anything unhealthy in your reactions, just bear in mind that sickness is the means by which an organism frees itself from what is alien; so one must simply help it to be sick, to have its whole sickness and to break out with it, since that is the way it gets better."[3]

In October, I wrote in my journal, "I've got to deal with my own shadow that trips me up and not be unfriendly or aloof to others, which was based on my insecurity and my old negative father complex. I needed to let myself and others see my new ego-Self connection, my true Self, and my union with anima (soul)."

At that time, Debbie and I were very close and it perplexed me how she could be so distant at times and so intimate at others. However, I always took solace in Jung's concept of "the tension of opposites." Looking back, it seems important to be with someone who has the same philosophy as you do. For instance, I feel that way currently in my relationship with Lanara.

Reflecting on my past two marriages, the first was a mistake based on an adolescent romantic love. Lynn, my first wife, was a very attractive and talented young actress. I met her in the theatre at Whittier College. She was the star of Bye Bye Birdie, and I had a small part as mayor. We started dating and eventually got married against my parents' advice. But, I was young and naive and unaware of her propensity to not be satisfied with one relationship. The marriage fell apart when she became involved with another man.[4]

---

3. Rilke, Rainer Maria. *Letters to a Young Poet*, 8.
4. See Rosen, D.H. (2014). *Lost in the Long White Cloud: Finding My Way*

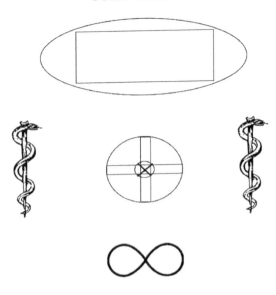

On November 8th, I thought about these images. The top figure is a rectangle representing the masculine inside an oval representing the feminine. Below it is a mandala representing wholeness and the feminine, and inside the circle is a cross, representing the integration of both male and female. This is also reflected in the bottom infinity drawing. Depicted on the sides are caduceus figures, representing healing.

It's clear that I was involved in integrating both parts of myself, which is a healing activity. It's noteworthy that at this time I was working on a book, *Transforming Depression*, that speaks to the same issue.

I dreamt that I was with an older Jewish man in New York. I found out that in his family, a young woman had died, which saddened me.

In reflecting on this dream, I was working on my father complex. It always distresses me when I think about my poor father being in the Navy, but advancing with the Marines to a remote island in the

Home. Eugene, OR: Wipf and Stock.

Pacific. By being in this kind of situation, his inner anima or soul was injured. I realize this affected me deeply. My father was a very sensitive person and my godfather, his dear friend, Sam Silverman, told me at his funeral that he was a physician, but also an artist.

Watercolor of Dogwood by my father

This etching by my mother underscores that both my parents were creative artists.

At this time I was in the final year of training to become an analyst, and was working on in-depth cases to complete my exams. I also used these same cases in my book, *Transforming Depression*. In retrospect, I realize that all writing is autobiographical. Through this creative effort, I was transforming my own depression and healing my soul through creativity, which is the actual subtitle of the book.

> Slowing down
> the pond's longer
> circle

Another dream fragment occurred on November 30th. I was a passenger in a car with Debbie. She was driving in a snow storm and veered off the road.

As is obvious, I pay serious attention to dreams. I wasn't quite sure whether or not I should interpret this as a bad omen forecasting difficulty in our marriage, but it got my attention and brought to light that I wasn't feeling safe in the relationship.

December 1st heralded Hanukkah, which is the bringing of light. At this time in my journal, I noted down a dream that I was presenting my work at the Esalen Retreat Center in Big Sur, California. *Stanislav Grof, a well-known psychiatrist and writer, was there and said, "You've discovered a conjunctive archetype of the bonding of the sexes and attachment to others." Later, I walked into the wilderness and over a mountain to a Buddhist retreat center. I got there without a problem, but then I wondered, 'How do I get back?'*

By writing the book on depression, I was overcoming my darkness by welcoming the light. Part of the healing involved going to Esalen and meeting Stan Grof as well as Joseph Campbell, author of *The Hero with a Thousand Faces.*[5] I was particularly struck by Camp-

5. Campbell, J. (1949). *The Hero with a Thousand Faces.* New York:

bell, this larger than life boy scout figure. He seemed incredibly good natured, competent, and kind. Following this experience, his book became a model for my and many people's healing journeys.

On December 9th, I dreamt that I was lost and alone in London. I met a young man, who was very happy. We walked into a building and he asked me to climb out on a ledge. I said, "No, I won't do that." There was a woman behind me who also said, "No, don't do it."

I felt that I was lost, both personally with my marital situation, and professionally, in that I felt alone with Jung. I couldn't talk with my wife about my professional isolation because she didn't like Jung. It seemed to me that she did not appreciate my wanting to be a Jungian analyst, which was distressing.

At this time, Verena Kast's book, *Joy, Inspiration, and Hope*, was published, based on her Fay lectures from the year before. This book was popular and well-reviewed. For example, Norman Cousins, author of *Head First: The Biology of Hope*, commented, "The book combines superb content with literary quality. In fact, just in the act of reading the book you experience the very emotions identified in the title. Kast contributes so handsomely to the means by which human beings can profit from important aspects of their uniqueness."[6]

Pantheon Books.

6. See Katz, V. (1991). *Joy, Inspiration, and Hope*. College Station: Texas A&M University Press.

Joy, Inspiration, and Hope

Verena Kast
TRANSLATED BY DOUGLAS WHITCHER
FOREWORD BY DAVID H. ROSEN

Cover of *Joy, Inspiration, and Hope*

I recall when Verena was at our home, she asked Debbie about Jung and the importance of what I was doing in the area of depression and egocide as an alternative to suicide. Debbie responded that she wasn't aware of what I was involved in, and this surprised Verena. She was so concerned that she later talked to me about it.

Chapter 12: Transforming Depression and Healing the Soul

Creativity is contagious.

—ALBERT EINSTEIN

I dreamt that Debbie and I were learning how to ski in a small place in Switzerland. We were on a high slope and there were more mountains and slopes in the background. We were skiing and Debbie fell and hurt herself. I also fell, but wasn't hurt.

Then a following dream fragment was of meeting a strong and young, attractive Chinese-American woman. We were intimate.

The initial dream indicated difficulty in my marriage and forecast a coming sabbatical in Switzerland. The second dream suggested union with my anima, creative self, as I was writing a proposal for a new book, *The Tao of Jung.* I was also drawn to the East, and in 1993, I went to Japan to give a lecture at the invitation of Hayao Kawai, who gave future Fay lectures on *Buddhism and the Art of Psychotherapy* in Texas.[1] Hayao Kawai was a very special person. When visiting to give lectures, he preferred humble accommodations at my house to the fancier Hilton hotel. He also befriended

1. Kawai, H. (1996). *Buddhism and the Art of Psychotherapy.* College Station, TX: Texas A&M University Press.

my youngest daughter, Rachel who played the cello. Later, when I visited Japan with my three daughters, he thoughtfully asked Rachel to accompany him on the cello while he played the flute for an auditorium full of Japanese researchers and staff. He was very humble. On one of our walks in Texas, when discussing our work as analysts, he said, "Do you have this experience? When I am seeing an analysand, I just sit there. I say nothing and do nothing. I am like a stone, and yet people pay me for that." I said, "I know exactly what you mean."

Rilke once wrote, "It seems to me that almost all our sadnesses are moments of tension, which we feel as paralysis because we no longer hear our astonished emotions living. Because we are alone with the unfamiliar presence that has entered us; because everything we trust and are used to is for a moment taken away from us; because we stand in the midst of a transition where we cannot remain standing. That is why the sadness passes: the new presence inside us, the presence that has been added, has entered our heart, has gone into its innermost chamber and is no longer even there, is already in our bloodstream. And we don't know what it was. We could easily be made to believe that nothing happened, and yet we have changed, as a house that a guest has entered changes. We can't say who has come, perhaps we will never know, but many signs indicate that the future enters us in this way in order to be transformed in us, long before it happens."[2]

In 1992, I completed the book manuscript for *Transforming Depression*, and Tarcher, an independent press, was going to publish it. Tarcher was bought by Putnam and I got a call from a senior editor at Tarcher, Connie Zweig. She informed me about the purchase and told me that I would need to rewrite my manuscript to make it accessible to the general public. I responded, "I don't know how to do that." She told me to come out to Los Angeles to edit the book with her. She helped a lot. However, I was distraught that all my

2. Rilke, Rainer Maria. *Letters to a Young Poet*, 8.

precious words were lost forever, but she reassured me that I could use them for another book. We finished the new version of *Transforming Depression*, which would be published by Putnam in 1993. Connie's excitement was infectious and it encouraged me to continue writing.

Third Edition of *Transforming Depression*

Because of the marital difficulty, Debbie and I went to see a therapist. I felt like we'd end up divorcing and we both got into some genuine pain regarding her mother. It was sad. Both of us were hesitant about getting a divorce, and Rob, our therapist, encouraged us to get on the train of marriage-improvement. We both decided to do so and give it 100%. Our goal was to not blame each other for any problems, have no depression, and just love and support one another.

This was a difficult time for my family. Rachel was 8, Laura 11, and Sarah 16. Our family center was not holding. Sarah was away at a camp and Laura was ill and losing weight. There was also no intimacy or closeness between Debbie and I. There seemed to be chaos in the house with little to no communication or interaction between us. She would take her things to the cleaners and leave mine behind. When I asked her about it, she seemed irritated, detached, and distant.

Debbie would often leave in the early morning before the kids left for school. She was never clear whether or not this was for work. I ended up making sure they had their breakfast and dropped them off. This part has never made any sense to me. I understand why our relationship would be troubling, and why she might put distance between us. But it seemed strange to put our daughters in our position. To me, Debbie not only seemed distant, but also depressed.

At this time, things were difficult and extremely busy for me. I had just officially become a Jungian analyst and received congratulatory calls from Peter Rutter, a Jungian analyst and colleague in Medicine, and John Beebe, also a respected Jungian analyst. John was the second Fay Lecturer and a gifted philosophical writer.[3]

3. Beebe, J. (1992). *Integrity in Depth*. College Station, TX: Texas A&M University Press.

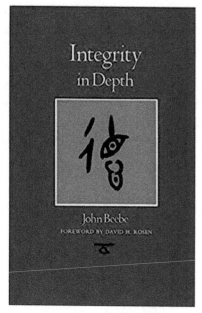

Cover of *Integrity in Depth*

I would often take walks with Rachel. She had the ability to tell a story and keep it going. I would ask her about one of the characters and she would pick up right where it left off. It's no surprise she's now writing her own book and has co-authored a new version of my first manuscript with me.[4]

A subsequent dream of Marion Woodman and Robert Bly (who used to give joint workshops). They asked me why Debbie was so depressed.

Of course, I have to own my individual anima. The dream question Marion and Robert were asking was why was *I* so depressed.

---

4. Rosen, D.H. and R. Rosen (2019). Lesbianism, A Study in Female Homosexuality—with a new Father-Daughter Dialogue. Eugene, OR: Wipf & Stock.

In early April 1993, Marion came to give the Fay Lectures on *The Stillness Shall Be the Dancing*.[5] Both my mother, Barbara, and my youngest sister, Nancy, came to College Station to hear her talks. The room was so crowded that the fire marshall came and said, "No more people can come in." Marion's talks covered the Great Mother and Father, the Black Madonna, the death and rebirth process, and T.S. Eliot's poem, "East Coker" from *The Four Quartets*. She was inspirational, upbeat, and involved the audience.

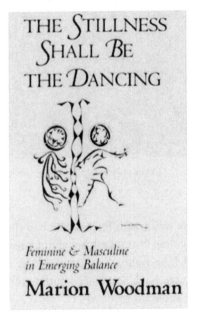

THE STILLNESS
SHALL BE
THE DANCING

*Feminine & Masculine
in Emerging Balance*

Marion Woodman

Cover of *The Stillness Shall Be the Dancing*

Even though I was having some difficulty and hopelessness in my marriage, I was also surrounded by so many smart and strong women kin, including my daughters, brilliant Fay lecturers, and my sister and mother. So while there was trouble in the forest, there were also angels.

5. Woodman, M. (1994). *The Stillness Shall Be the Dancing: Feminine & Masculine in Emerging Balance*. College Station, TX: Texas A&M University Press.

Wind in the pines
angels whispering

Chapter 13: Living in Switzerland

David's painting of Santorini, Greece

We must be able to let things happen in the psyche. For us, this actually is an art of which few people know anything. Consciousness is forever interfering, helping, correcting, and negating, and never leaving the simple growth of the psychic processes in peace. It would be simple enough, if only simplicity were not the most difficult of all things.

—CARL GUSTAV JUNG

I dreamt I was in the Swiss Alps and the snow was melting. It was beautiful. I was with Debbie.

Some dreams are self-explanatory. This was prophetic because I was going to Switzerland on sabbatical, although, alas, Debbie chose not to come with me.

In 1994, before going to Europe, I visited my sister Marti and her husband Larry in Ponca, Arkansas. We visited a lovely natural place, Steel Creek in the Ozark Mountains. We hiked a trail and the bluffs were majestic. We walked through Lost Valley and on to some falls by the Eden Caves.

Falling water
beams of light
bursts of green buds

Tall lone red cedar
on cliff rock
overlooking Eden Falls

Going from a mildly southern state to a civilized, European nation was just the right move. Spending a fair amount of time in the country where Carl Jung was born and raised was particularly exciting. I found an apartment to rent in Bassersdorf because the owner was going to study meditation in Thailand. This village was typically Swiss, with beautiful parks and a river running through it. This allowed me to live and work in a fully furnished apartment, which had a lovely view of the forest and hills in that area. I came to Switzerland to do research for a book I was writing on Jung's life, called *The Tao of Jung: The Way of Integrity.*[1] I interviewed people who knew Jung well and worked closely with him, for example C.A. Meier and Marie-Louis von Franz. I also interviewed Jung's only son, Franz, who lived in his parent's home, a beautiful and stately place on Zurich Lake. He and others were extremely

1. Rosen, D.H. (1996). *The Tao of Jung: The Way of Integrity*. New York: Viking Penguin.

helpful. Magically, I had stumbled on the title for my book, which was mirrored back to me when I attended the Antioch Writer's Conference.[2] One of the writer instructors had said, "You're onto something. You'll sell the book because of this title." I was shocked by this, but went with it, and the instructor was right.

When I was writing *The Tao of Jung* on my sabbatical in Switzerland during 1994, I interviewed Aniela Jaffe, Jung's secretary and a Jungian analyst in her own right. She was the person behind *Memories, Dreams, Reflections.* Aniela was very gracious and kind. I met her because of the fact that she was Jewish and Jung helped her get out of Nazi Germany. This was good news to me, as it dispelled myths that Jung was anti-Semitic. I then wrote an article about Jung and Judaism, which allowed me to go forward.[3]

Aniela Jaffe

2. This was the only writer's conference I ever attended, but it was well worth it.

3. Rosen, D.H. (1996). If only Jung had had a Rabbi. *The Journal of Analytical Psychology,* 41, 245–256.

I also met and talked with Jung's son, Franz, in his father's office. He was sitting in the very place that Jung sat in the well-known photograph (shown below). We talked about the Red Book. He pointed to a tall shelf and said, "There it is." I asked if the book would be released and he said, "No. My father didn't want it published."[4] Franz also asked if I'd like to see an engraved piece of marble that his father had made. We went to the basement and he showed it to me. I noticed that it was chipped on one corner. He explained, "We found this by a huge gingko tree that the American students at the Institute had given him as a memorial to Emma, who died in 1955. It was chipped by a lawnmower but otherwise intact." The engraving was of falling leaves from a gingko tree. On the bottom were Chinese characters that read, "Emma lived in moderation."[5]

In the summer of 1994, Debbie and my three daughters were going to visit me in Bassersdorf. We were going to take an extended vacation in Italy and Greece. It was a surprise when my three daughters arrived in Switzerland during the summer without their mother. I asked, "Why didn't she come? She was supposed to be here." They said that she wanted to be by herself. I was confused and concerned by this. I couldn't understand why she wouldn't come with our daughters. This eventually led to a divorce orchestrated by her.

To say the least, this was a difficult time for me and my daughters. Though Debbie and I had talked about separation or even divorce, I thought the old adage must be true with me being in Switzerland: "Distance makes the heart grow fonder." I never imagined such a traumatic separation was in the making.

---

4. Later the Jung family published this book. See Jung, Carl G. *The Red Book: Liber Novus.* Ed. by Sonu Shamdasani. New York & London: W.W. Norton & Company, 2009.

5. I later read in Catrine Clay's *Labyrinths* that the engraving was really about Tony Wolf. See Clay, C. (2016). *Labyrinths: Emma Jung, Her Marriage to Carl, and the Early Years of Psychoanalysis.* New York: HarperCollins.

Carl Jung in his office

My oldest daughter, Sarah, was 18 and about to begin her studies at the University of Texas in Austin. My middle daughter, Laura, was 13, which we all know is one of the most difficult periods in life. My youngest daughter, Rachel, was only 10. I know this was an extremely challenging time for all of them.

After six months, when my sabbatical was over, I returned home from Switzerland. I then went to North Dakota to give an invited talk on my book, *Transforming Depression: Healing the Soul Through Creativity*. While there, I visited the Badlands and forded the tiny beginning of the Missouri River. Crossing the river I reached a plateau, where there were grazing cows and a rainbow. I was beginning to realize the value of depression and how that energy can be transformed into creativity. I was practicing what I preached.

> Burning candles
> light in the darkness. . .
> hope in the Badlands

Chapter 14: The End is the Beginning

"Marvelous truth, confront us at every turn in every guise"

—DENISE LEVERTOV

I dreamt of leaving my mother's house. I moved out from Debbie's and lived in my mother's old house. My father lived across the street. Finally I'd be on my own! Debbie was with a man that was a friend of mine from medical school. They kissed. Then the man blessed me as I left, saying "Go as you'd like others to know you."

In 1995, on my return to Texas, I entered one of the most difficult periods of my life. I was prepared for repair and continuation of my marriage, but what I ended up dealing with was the way that my negative anima and mother complex manifested within my relationship. This led to a lot of healing in my own therapy as I sought out positive anima figures. For example, I saw a female Kleinian analyst. Melanie Klein was the founder of object relations and spoke of symbolism of breasts, including good breasts (referring to a kind maternal and nurturing figure) and bad breasts (referring to an unkind and less nurturing feminine figure).

Standing in front of the Brazos County Courthouse with Debbie on Halloween, little did I know the extent of that archetypal trick-or-treat. Now, I thank my ex-wife for divorcing me, as I never would have met Lanara, my lovely wife.

After Debbie and I divorced, I recalled that she never quite fit in with my parents, who had had some reservations that I had not previously understood. I am leaving out the exact events that precipitated Debbie's and my divorce, which were far more complicated and painful than her simply not coming to Switzerland. I have long wrestled with pain and anguish over this incident and our relationship, and with the fact that, as so often happens in divorces, my daughters were caught in the middle. But by intensive in-depth analytic therapy, I grew to accept and transform this tragic situation. And the process of writing this memoir, and facing my life, has helped me to further let go.

I was invited to Bismarck, North Dakota to give a talk regarding *Transforming Depression.* I was the guest of the Touch the Earth Educational Center. Following that, in August of 1995, I was invited to give a talk on depression and suicide, which are generally neglected topics in analytic psychology. It was a presentation at the International Congress for Analytical Psychology, in Zurich, Switzerland. The end of the year was filled with fun travels to Canada, Arizona, Louisiana, and Tennessee to give lectures. Better to be invited and lauded and traveling, than spend time at home dealing with rejection and depression. Also, I found the nature in those states so healing and comforting.

High on the hill

smile on its face,

a cougar

At the end of that year, I met a female professor in another department. She had a stunning name which accompanied her physical loveliness. She was a refugee, with memories of leaving the country when a dictator came to power. She enjoyed traveling, and we visited many national parks together. She was a good companion, very bright, and loved nature and creativity. Had it been a different time in my life, had I been a bit more free of the pain from my previous marriage, we would have certainly married and had a family. But as it was, we simply had a wonderful few years together.

Chapter 15: Living Alone

How clear it is! How quiet it is! It must be something eternally existing!

—LAO TZU

I dreamt I was going back to nature. Hayao Kawai was in it. The dream was very peaceful and involved water and a quartet of writers.

In 1996, during my visits to Japan, Hayao Kawai was an important figure. In fact, after giving his Fay Lectures, he remained a dear friend and colleague.[1] He was the director of the International Research Center for Japanese Studies and later became a Minister of Culture in the Japanese government.

I traveled back to Ponca, Arkansas since I enjoyed the rest and relaxation while visiting my sister, Marti, and her husband, Larry. I returned to the Lost Valley, which is near where she lives. In mid March, I wrote these two haiku.

Grey clouds
and drizzle. . .
walking into Lost Valley

1. Hayao Kawai, 1996. Buddhism and the art of Psychotherapy. Texas A&M University Press.

In retracing our previous steps, we headed back to the caves I loved.

Near Eden Falls
inside a huge, womblike cave
looking out, nature found

There was a major thunder and lightening storm during my trip. After the storm, it was refreshing and there was blue sky. It was so peaceful visiting my sister and her family. We enjoyed many quiet breakfasts of organic raisin bran, bananas, orange juice and fresh coffee. Marti shared Bill Moyers' *Language of Life* with me. She wanted me to read a poem by Naomi Shehab Nye. Nye had a few phrases that stuck in my mind, like, "We are forever searching" and her favorite quote, which comes from Thailand, "Life is so short we must move very slowly." I thought to myself that poems help us to do just that, by allowing us to savor a single image or phrase. This is one of Nye's vital poems:

The Art of Disappearing

When they say Don't I know you?
say no.
When they invite you to the party
remember what parties are like
before answering.
Someone telling you in a loud voice
they once wrote a poem.
Greasy sausage balls on a paper plate.
Then reply.

If they say We should get together
say why?

It's not that you don't love them anymore.
You're trying to remember something
too important to forget.
Trees. The monastery bell at twilight.
Tell them you have a new project.
It will never be finished.

When someone recognizes you in a grocery store
nod briefly and become a cabbage.
When someone you haven't seen in ten years
appears at the door,
don't start singing him all your new songs.
You will never catch up.

Walk around feeling like a leaf.
Know you could tumble any second.
Then decide what to do with your time.

In the book, Nye says to Moyers, "I guess I have an obsession with disappearing. Maybe that's why I love the subtlety of Japanese poetry so much. I love that understatement which is a powerful part of Japanese culture." Then she talked about the art and process of writing, "Through the process of writing, things are given back to me, just by writing it. I think that will happen for everybody who opens that writing door."[2] I guess this is what this process of writing memoirs has done for me, as well. It has given so much back to me.

Being a single father with two growing daughters was a lot to handle. Naively, I agreed to an 80/20 split with my ex-wife getting 80 percent of the time with my daughters. But, I felt that this was

2. Moyers, Bill. 1995. *The Language of Life: A Festival of Poets*. New York: Doubleday Books. 329.

wrong, so I hired a lawyer and went to court. Fortunately, the judge granted a 50/50 arrangement, which I think was in everyone's best interest. I recall once driving Laura and Rachel over to their mother's house. Laura didn't want to get out of the car because she was struggling to accept her mother's new partner. When I asked why, she responded, "I only like you as my father."

At home, I became both father and mother to my kids. I learned to cook.[3] I continued to paint for my mental health. I also kept teaching and seeing analytic patients. This was a time when I had an agent and published paperback versions of *Transforming Depression* and *The Tao of Jung*.

Enzo drawing by me

I later dreamt that I was taking a trout to a couple who were the parents of a young woman who would take and raise the fish. They lived on the Gulf of Mexico. It was a long journey.

---

3. See my cookbook, published in 2017: Rosen, D.H. 2017. The Alchemy of Cooking: Recipes with a Jungian Twist. Eugene, OR: Wipf & Stock Press.

At this time, I was involved with the female professor mentioned earlier, whose parents lived along the Gulf of Mexico. She was a very creative and independent person, and seemed, in part, to represent my developing anima. At one point she asked how I got my endowed position. I explained that you simply apply for it when you see one advertised. She later acquired such a position at a major university.

During this year, I gave many lectures on transforming depression, W.B. Yeats' poem, "The Second Coming," and Toni Morrison's novel, *Beloved*.[4] I also returned to Touch the Earth Educational Center in Bismark, North Dakota to give a talk on *The Tao of Jung*. Additionally, I gave a presentation titled, "Don't Be Cruel to the Heart That's True: Understanding the King and What Went Wrong," at the Second Annual International Conference on Elvis Presley at the University of Mississippi in Oxford.[5]

While there, I went on a blind date with a woman from California. After she knocked and I opened the door, I quickly shut it because I couldn't believe such a beautiful woman would come to meet me in such a distant place. Realizing what I had done, I quickly opened the door again, apologized, and invited her in. My two years spent with her were exciting, educational, and at times quite tender.

Following this, I gave a professional lecture, which was also very personal, "The Self and Other Connection: The Relationship between Attachment Style, Capacity to Forgive, and Defense Style" at the American Psychological Association's Annual Meeting in Toronto, Canada. In mid-September I organized a conference on the "Evolution of the Psyche," hosted at Texas A&M. At that meeting, I spoke on "Evolutionary Memory." Later that month I gave

4. Just as I am writing this section, the world is mourning Morrison's recent death in August, 2019.

5. This paper would later be incorporated in a published book. See Rosen, D.H. 2002. The Tao of Elvis. Orlando: FL: Harcourt.

two more talks on "The Tao of Jung" and "Transforming Depression" in Portland, Oregon. The event was sponsored by the C.G. Jung Institute, Pacific Northwest, of which I'm now a member. For the rest of the year, I continued traveling to different cities across the U.S. to give lectures.

Chapter 16: Counting My Blessings

The sparrow is sorry for the peacock for the burden of his tail.

—RABINDRANATH TAGORE

In 1997, I had the idea of writing a novel.[1] These were my notes:

I'd fallen and hit my head, my second chakra, and broke my nose. I saw stars. It was an electric shock of sorts. It woke me up like I'd been asleep for years. Living out identities written for me in the archetypal unconscious.

I knew I was a wounded healer, no doubt. I had committed egocide and transformed my psyche several times. But now, with the blood gushing down my face, screaming, "Damn it! Take me to the hospital," I woke up after it was all said and done.

My third eye was open. The realization was upon me, 'Tell the truth and it will set you free.' It was all about my beginning. I was bred in Rye, but born in Port Chester, New York. Clearly I don't believe the adage that the pun is the lowest form of humor.

The house I was born and raised in was called "Bright Bank." It was an old mansion that was the home of the Civil War Union general,

1. This would not happen until much later, when I would write a historical novella about Opal Whitely.

Carlton. My parents bought it for cheap in the Depression. Little did I know that this was an omen of my future—of the wars that would divide parents and those that would divide myself and my former wives.

Looking back on the hectic pace of my life, I subconsciously must have realized that I was doing too much. In due course, this became a burden. I felt like I was in a long line, the kind your find at the post office, you're waiting forever, moving slowly, and talking to strangers only for a brief moment. However, at the time, I was barely conscious of this fact.

Post office. . .
long lines
short chats

I began the year with an invited lecture and workshop presentation at the Center for Jungian Studies in South Florida, followed by a presentation on my books in Dallas, and of course, in College Station, where I had organized the Brazos Valley Jungian Society.

I ventured to New York City to attempt to find a recording contract for Miranda Zent, a singer I managed back in College Station. She was a student in the Psychology of Religion class, and asked me if she could sing her presentation rather than write a paper. I said she could if she wrote down the song and explained it. I was so impressed by her song, "Sweet Renunciation," that I thought she could make a record. I was shocked by how poor, rundown, and unprofessional the recording people were. It reminded me of how it must have been to contact mafia people. Obviously, it didn't work out for a record contract, but Miranda remained a prominent singer in plays at Texas A&M. She later got an assistant-ship in theater at a major university.[2]

2. If you are interested in hearing this song, you can still hear sound clips of Miranda's work and this song atat reverbnation. https://www.reverbnation.com/mirandazent/songs.

Chapter 16: Counting My Blessings

Looking back on my life, I am reminded of my many blessings.

1. *Sarah, my oldest daughter, who is quiet, sensitive, gentle, and honest.*

2. *Laura, my middle daughter, who is ambitious, beautiful, intelligent, and a doer.*

3. *Rachel, my youngest daughter, who is a natural-born leader, as well as a kind, giving person.*

4. *The beautiful woman from California whom I called, "The Golden Woman."*

5. *Tao, Sarah's black lab, who was friendly and loyal.*

6. *Abby, Laura's dog, a younger black lab, who was mischieveous and friendly.*

7. *Becky, Rachel's basset hound, who was sweet and yielding.*

8. *My mother, Barbara, very creative, giving, and loving.*

9. *My aunt, Martha, my mother's only sibling, kind and practical.*

10. *My sister, Janet, who is very patient, raises beautiful orchids, and raised five gifted sons.*

11. *My sister, Marti, wedded to the Earth, who helped save the Buffalo River in Arkansas.*

12. *My sister, Nancy, an editor, both loving and creative, she sheperded many books.*

13. *My physician brother, Bill, who has a heart for healing the elderly.*

14. *My health, or at least my persistance in making the best of life despite illness.*

15. *My artistic ability through painting and poetry.*

16. *My writing of books.*

17. *My abilities as a healer (physician, psychiatrist, and analyst).*

18. *My ability to teach and love it.*

19. *My past and future travels.*

20. *My capacity to keep and maintain friendships.*

21. *My home in the country, surrounded by forrest.*

22. *My job.*

23. *My spiritual development, combining Eastern and Western philosophy.*

24. *My ability to recall dreams.*

25. *My nature to daydream.*

26. *A love of walking.*

27. *My fondness for trees, plants, and flowers.*

28. *The sun on my face.*

29. *Rain and showers.*

30. *Managing a singer, which is a reflection of my helping others to be authentic.*

31. *Mid-wife to the Fay Lectures and Books.*

32. *Massage receiver and giver.*

33. *Being and giving love.*

34. *Hope, joy, and faith always.*

35. *Optimism.*

36. *Valuing life and its sacredness.*

37. *Music.*

38. *Manifesting my five senses—seeing, hearing, smelling, touching, tasting.*

39. *My sixth sense, intuition.*

40. *Cooking.*

41. *My Greek family.*

42. *Soul—inner and outer.*

43. *Friends in Japan, England, Switzerland, Italy, Brazil, and China.*

44. *Ice cream—especially, Coconut Bliss.*

45. *Good coffee.*

46. *Love and marriage.*

47. *Good home and parents.*

48. *Striving for practicality.*

49. *The years spent with and the memory of our dog Willow.*

50. *Our new dog, Willa, and the years together still to come.*

The Fay Lectures in Analytical Psychology were going well. This year welcomed *Gender & Desire: Uncursing Pandora* by Polly Young-Eisendrath.[3]

I continued my research on depression and suicide. A piece by this title was published in *Open Questions in Analytical Psychology*.

A very important program on Jung and China occured with Murry Stein and Heyong Shen at the Jung Institute of Chicago. My part was on "The Tao of Jung: The Way of Integrity." I then gave a presentation on "Measurement of Jungian Personality Typology" with one of my graduate students, R.C. Arnau, and a faculty member, B. Thompson. I then gave two lectures on "Transforming Depression and the Meaning of Suicide" at Osaka and Kyoto Bunkyo Universities in Japan. I continued to give talks on "Psychology and Spirituality: Eastern and Western Influences." In Houston, I gave a presentation, titled, "The Myth of Elvis Lives On." As the year came to a close, I lectured on "The Tao of Jung" and "Transforming Depression" at Common Boundary's 17th Annual Conference on "Creativity, Imagination, and Healing" in Washington, D.C.

3. Young-Eisendrath, P. 1997. Gender & Desire: Uncursing Pandora. College Station, TX: Texas A&M University Press.

Even though I had ended the previous year saying that I would travel less and committ myself to fewer obligations, I clearly did not follow through on that.

Chapter 17: Year of the Tiger

The gladdest moment in human life, me thinks, is a departure into unknown lands.

—SIR RICHARD BURTON

A huge turtle was trying to get out of the back gate. My brother, Bill, was in the yard. I yell, "it's getting out" but I couldn't stop it. It comes out and walks toward me and turns into a man. I think to myself, "Oh my god! A turtle man!"

This dream represents my shadow. In general, the shadow is often the opposite of the positive ego; it is frequently a reflection of the repressed part of oneself. The challenge is to embrace that part of oneself. In dreams, the shadow is often represented by a member of one's own sex: when a man dreams of another man, it is often his shadow. Characteristically, one's shadow relates to the parent complex, and in the case of my dream, a father complex. The issue I was wrestling with was the challenge to "be my brother's keeper," as the saying goes. By being challenged to embrace my brother, who is very much *like* my father, I was also being led to accept my *father* and that aspect of myself. Both Bill and the turtle man represent my male shadow: so I need to deal with my slowness and my hard shell. Both of these are true of me. I have a lot of defenses, and am a very quiet but deliberate being. I advance slowly but surely, like the turtle from the story of the turtle and the hare.

I was up at four a.m. for the long trek to China, fulfilling a boyhood dream of mine. I had planned to go to China in the Fall of 1989, but cancelled because of the Tiananmen Square incident. Now after so much water has gone under the bridge, like Clinton who visited China earlier that year (in 1998), I too forgave what had happened. After leaving from Vancouver, I arrived in Hong Kong after a fourteen hour flight. Then I hurried through customs and was helped by a female worker for Japan Airlines. I then got on a China Southern Flight, which left at eight p.m. for Guangzhou.

Hong Kong was new, huge, shiny, and clearly British. The contrast was so striking. When I arrived in Guangzhou, it was nearly nine p.m. I was immediately hit by the third world nature of the airport and city. There was dirt, chaos, and plastic everywhere. There were tons of people in disorder. It was poor, busy, dusty, and had the feeling of being in Mexico. For example, at the currency exchange, the woman in charge made me sign a paper four times to make sure my signature matched the one on my passport. I was exhausted and suffering from jetlag.

I was met by three students around age 20. They were Gao Lan's students, the wife of Heyong Shen, and Professor of Child Development. One of the students, named Apple, was the organizer. She held up a sign, which I recognized immediately. It said, "First International Conference of Jungian Psychology and Chinese Culture." We got in a taxi, but had to get out quickly because a policeman made us, saying the taxi was in the wrong spot. We drove a long way on crowded, bumpy, and dusty roads. We were accompanied by a second student named Egg. What a ride!

We went to a seafood restaurant. I had to lug my big suitcase upstairs while we ate shrimp cakes, pork pies, egg rolls, rice soup with sliced fish (yum), and custard pies, along with oolong tea. It was like a dream when we entered the restaurant. There were tanks of live waterbeetles, turtles, eels, and all kinds of fish. They said, "Pick out what you want." I was repulsed by the waterbeetles, turtles, and eels, so I chose the fish. I did eat a little bit of eel several times and it was good.

Following this, we went to the Academic Exchange Center at South China Normal University. It was a kind of campus hotel. Heyong came by to say hi. The university overlooked a pond. It was a tropical climate and there were palm trees and many flowers with violet, orchid-like blooms—beautiful. They did have an interesting and compassionate custom: there was a little dish in the corner of the bedroom with food on it. This was for mice and rats so they wouldn't bother the people.

Back at my hotel, and after a bath, I went to sleep at midnight. I was totally spent. I woke up in the early morning, a bit jetlegged. Then I finally got up at seven a.m. All sorts of people were up and out already. It was a hazy morning and all the locals were doing tai chi, pelvic thrusts, and jogging using very little steps, as though they were jogging in slow motion. I wondered if this was a common form of exercise and later learned that it was a part of Chinese culture.

Heyong Shen, whom I had befriended at a meeting in Chicago the year before and who organized the conference, wanted to become a Jungian analyst. It was obvious he loved Jung and later did become an analyst—the first Jungian analysit in China, actually—after completing his training in the C.G. Jung institute in San Francisco.

I went to breakfast with John Beebee, a Jungian analyst that I knew from prior training in San Francisco. After breakfast, we toured Guangzhou. We then visited a Taoist temple that was nearby. Later, we went to a shopping mall with a huge Santa Claus outside. Guangzhou was Western, like Hong Kong. For lunch, we met up with Heyong and went to a restaurant, where I ordered honey melon and watermelon. Interestingly, it came cut up in pieces and served in milk with ice cubes, which was unexpected but tasty. Then we went to a huge, government owned, bookstore. There were Mao's books. We saw a new mandala series, which were Jungian books published by The People's Publishing House. I was struck by the Jungian books and asked how it was possible to publish his books in China. Heyong responded, "Jung said, 'Serve the People and Community.'" This sentiment resonated strongly with Chinese values.

The next day, after a quick breakfast of hot rice cereal (which reminded me of oatmeal), Heyong asked if I found the treasures in it—boiled egg, vegetables, and meat. And I said, "Yes. Thank you. This makes it very unique and creative." We then walked to the conference room together.

The conference was historic. Heyong gave a wonderful talk about how Jung's psychology was perfect for China. Even though I knew that Jung had visited China at one point, I was still pleasantly surprised by the fact that Heyong had learned about him and that Jung was being mentioned in psychology in China. Afterward, both John Beebee and I gave talks. Beebee's talk was personal, as he was born in China. I gave a talk on the tradition of Tao, spefically the Tao of Jung, which was eventually translated into Chinese. After a tea break, Stan Marlan gave a lecture on an ancient Taoist priest. Following this, there was another banquet that had the best food I've ever had. It was the peak of a dining experience, with multiple, state of the art dishes, the likes of which I had never before experienced. I thought to myself, "boy, they really know how to cook and eat well."

I met the editor of the mandala series, as they were going to translate my book, *The Tao of Jung*, and several volumes of the Fay book series into Chinese.

Heyong Shen told me about his philosophy of heart psychology. He mentioned that on a train ride from St. Louis to Los

Angeles, he once dreamt that he took his head off and put it on the table, and he could still see. He said, "I guess I was too much in my head. Now I'm focusing on psychology of the heart."

After several other talks, we toured temples in Guangzhou. Then, as usual, we went to a restaurant. We could pick and choose from the following: ginger soup, 1,000 year old eggs, fresh snails, crab, shrimp, vegetables, and noodles.

Part of the tour was visiting Guo'en Temple, the birthplace of the sixth patriarch, Hui Neng. He was the founder of Chan Buddhism, the forerunner of Zen Buddhism. I was pleased to learn that all of the male leaders were infused with feminine energy from Quan Yin, who looks exactly like the Virgin Mary. At this temple we were served a vegetarian meal by the monks.

Later I took a long walk with Heyong. I underscored that he was and is a pioneer, and that Jung's psychology was a perfect match for China. Already he talked about a second international conference, which he wanted to be on the *I-Ching*. I brainstormed about my research on the psychology of Haiku in Japan, which took me back to Chinese poets, for haiku originated in China. We discussed how the *I-Ching* was really about poetry and the essence of haiku. Then I bought Heyong a drink of pure malt whiskey. We toasted to the great success of his first international conference.

I loved the trips after the talks. For example, we visited the Seven Star Crags. It was by a peaceful lake. It reminded me of the many chinese paintings I had seen over the years, with stunning mountains coming out of blue waters. Then I realizeed where the paintings came from. I hadn't realized, until that moment that China was so, so beautiful. It was simply magical. As I was often prone to do, I went off by myself and saw a gallery of 1,000 years of poets. The walls were covered with poems. I had never been in anything like it. I wrote two haiku there.

Torn Asunder

Banyan-rooted rock cave
1,000 year old poets
butterfly glides silently

Seven star crags emerge
from jade water
gold fish at bottom

Today China awakens! As Napolean said about China, "There lies a sleeping giant."

At the end of the conference, John Beebee gave a closing talk based on Hexagram #45, "Gathering Together." It emphasizes gathering strength to defend against unforeseen things. We must make conscious what is hidden in the unconscious.

During one of our meals, a Chinese student of herbal medicine looked at my palms. She said, "You are healthy." She then took my pulse in left and right wrists and said that my heart is my weakest organ and that I should meditate more. This would decrease stress and increase rest and relaxation. She explained, "It's hard to grow up holistic and we must separate out and become individualistic. You grew up separate, and you must become holistic." She said, "Our country is very progressive because of the Communist government. We have food, consumer products, free education, health care, no guns, and virtually no drugs or crime. We have more freedom than ever."

I went to a restaurant to have Chrysanthemum tea—a first, and quite tasty. Then I flew to Beijing and was met by a tour guide, Mr. Lee, who took me to a palace hotel. It was hazy and drizzling. Part of the arranged tour was to go to a jade factory. Jade is a symbol of everlasting love. I called Heyong's aunt and uncle and arranged to have dinner with them. Heyong's brother picked me up at the hotel. We went to see the Forbidden City, or "Ch'chieng,"

Imperial Palace and Temple of Heaven, where the emperors of Ming and Ching dynasties prayed for good harvests. I ended up visiting the Summer Palace, a beautiful setting. I asked what the square was for and was told, "Earth and the male," and the circle, "Heaven and the female."

Heyong's brother, He Liang, picked me up for the long ride to visit Heyong's aunt and uncle. They were military officers and members of the Communist Party. The man was very tall, and was a former Army basketball player. They were very friendly. I was struck by the long walk up four flights of steps, as in this country we are so used to elevators which make us a bit lazy. We sat around their kitchen table. The food was all prepared—1,000 year-old eggs, pig liver, beef, vegetables, pork and noodles, and pickled vegetables. It was very tasty, with ample beer, and good conversation. His uncle had been to Canada and the United States. His work involved computers, and his wife, was a weather researcher with a government job. She underscored that it was a secure job and she received low cost housing and good benefits.

After all the propoganda I recieved in the U.S. about communism being evil, I learned that actually, China's having a free education and healthcare was a huge benefit both to individuals and the society.

Chapter 18: Japan (Nihon)

They are forever free who renounce all selfish desires and break away
from the ego-cage"

THE BHAGAVAD GITA, 2:54–65, 71–72

Drizzle—
star magnolia glistening

I was speaking with a woman on the telephone when a monarch butterfly landed on my left forearm. It stayed with me for a while. It looked at me and explored my skin. I was sitting on a deck with blue skies overhead.

A butterfly represents the soul and transformation. This is because how wonderous it seems that a caterpiller could go into a chrysalis and then come out as a butterfly. In my dream, the butterfly speaks to the necessity of creative quietude and incubation in the healing process. My anima (soul) or feminine side is represented by the woman I am speaking with. Through her, I am moved from what is patriarchal and technological, toward a grounding with the feminine (i.e. rest). By speaking with my anima I am speaking with myself about a coming transformation to take place during my pilgrimage to Japan. In other words I was going to stop and get off the merry-go-round.

In the year of 1999, Laura was at the University of Texas at Austin in their honors program, called Plan II. She was very gifted and intellectual, and had two majors: finance and government. When she graduated several years later, she recieved a Fullbright Scholarship to Peru. When she was a child, I always imagined she'd be a leader somehow. I have a vivid memory of her in elementary school jumping on the kitchen table and announcing "I am going to be president!" I still think she should be president!

This year was filled with more talks and a great many travels. In March of 1999, I gave more talks on the Tao of Elvis in New York and Missouri. I also gave a talk in Boston with Michale Luebbert on attachment and psychosocial development at the annual meating of the American Psychological Association.

From June until the end of the year, I went on a sabbatical to Japan. I went there do research on Haiku, their psychology, and meaning. But first I took a small vacation and tour of Japan with my three duaghters, Sarah, Laura, and Rachel. One of our first stops was at a Japanese inn, called a Ryokan. This was a traditional Japanese inn with the tatami-mat rooms, communal baths, women on one side and men on the other. The baths are called Onsens. We went to the botanical gardens in Kyoto and also to the Royal Palace Estate and Tea House. I also wanted my daughters to know about the hor-

Shadow burnt into wall—

Rain falls, leaving no sound
Behind

I wrote the above Haiku in order to deal with the angst I was feeling, and it is now published in my collection, *The Healing Spirit of Haiku.*

After our visit to the memorial we a restaurant in the town. With the images of America's violence so stark in my mind, I was embaressed and shameful to be American. I thought the townsfolk would be angry at us for destroying their city. But instead, in a Buddhist style, they were accepting and kind. My daughters seemed to deeply appreciate this trip, and were clearly moved by the experience.

Soon after my daughters returned to the United States I met Hiroshi Yokoyama in Kyoto. We had an elaborate ten course meal and sake and god knows how many beers. I really liked this individual and we had a wonderful time together. After learning that both of our fathers fought in world war two, he generously said, "My father and your father were enemies, but we are friends." It was one of those moments where both of us teared up.

Hiroshi was the primary translator of "Transforming Depression" into Japanese. He said he wrote an epilogue saying that my book was, "a cry from my soul." He thought it was important that the book adressed egocide, which was a timely concept because Japan was in the middle of an epidemic of suicides. Hiroshi was ecstatic that Hayao Kawai wrote the preface for the Japanese edition of the book. I think the book's importance in Japan is in part indebted to Kawai, as he later became a minister of culture. As an indicator of how beloved he was by Japanese people, when I visited Hayao and we when walked down the street together, people would bow to him.

While I was in Japan, in September, I gave a talk on "Transforming Depression" at the Tokyo Institue of Psychiatry. In November I gave another talk, "Surviving Suicidal Depression: Egocide and the Buddha at Konan University in Kobe." Because I had come to study Haiku, I was particularly delighted to give a special lecture entitled, "The Soul of Haiku: Its Psychology, Meaning, and Healing Value" at Kyoto Bunkyo University I also enjoyed giving several lectures on "The Tao of Jung" all over Japan, since it also had been translated into Japanese.

During this year, I was pleased that the book, *Evolution of the Psyche,* which I edited with Michael Luebbert, was finally published. This book resulted from a conference at which international and multi-disciplinary scholars presented on the theme of evolution of consciousness (both individual and social). In this volume, Holy Huston and I contributed an essay on evolutionary archetypal memory.

Despite continuing to give some academic lectures, I also utilized this time in Japan to rest and relax. I also wrote many Haiku, including the following:

Empty heart
full moon
tears flow

Soft touch of your fingers
on my warm face—
gentle mist

The first one reflects my loneliness and emptiness which was necessary for a spiritual experience. The second reflects the need we all have for relationship. The illustration below, which reminds me of my time in Japan, represents growth and development, as well as the necessity of being able to flow with life.

Chapter 19: Evolution of Self

"Please remember, it is what you are the heals, not what you know."

—CARL JUNG

I dreampt I no longer had to be in a mental hospital in Japan, as I was not suicidal any longer.

Japan was a time of healing, recovery, and ironically, a cessation of a stage in my life in which I needed to travel to other countries. I think that being alone and focusing on one thing—haiku—for months on end allowed my mind to rest and to no longer be stressed by the chaos of academia.

Sauntering
hollyhocks and marigolds
nodding

An additional and related dream had me returning to Shetland and climbing a mountain of hope.

This second dream also concerns travel, but takes me back to Shetland, where Sarah was born in 1976. It's likely that this mountain has to do with feeling hopeful about my oldest daughter and her future life. She ended up founding the Phoenix Center for Traumatized Youth in Marble Falls, Texas, which has been very successful!

This year, 2000, the first year of the new millenia, started off with my being asked to write a foreword to the Japanese edition of *Transforming Depression* which was titled in Japanese, *Living Through Depression: Healing of the Soul by Dreams and Paintings*. The principle translator was Yokoyama, though he had others helping as well. One of my favorite activities was coordinating the Fay Lectures and editing the books that followed. For example, in 2000 I was honored to write a forward to *The Archetypal Imagination* by James Hollis. Another enjoyable writing project was having an entry for Carl Gustav Jung put into the Encyclopedia of Psychology published by the American Psychological Association. I was delighted that Jung was being taken seriously academically.

I travelled to Rochester, New York to attend the memorial service for George Engel on January 29th. He had been an important mentor and friend. After the service, several close friends and colleagues gathered at the house of our mutual friend, Tim Quill. It was heartwarming to reflect on the virtues of such an important and caring physician as well as a delightful person. I was filled with memories of George walking me around his garden of roses, which he carefully tended. I also recalled that whenever anyone went to his house, he took pride in showing off his wife's paintings. He also loved to make tea on his own, gathering natural ingredients and steeping them for guests. For example, his blackberry tea was exceptional for its unique flavor and the care he put into it.

In my home life, things were in a new stage. My daughter Rachel was the only one still living with me, a burgeoning teenager at 16. I took my duties seriously, and would make delicious meals for us. For example, Rachel liked homemade soba vegetable soup, which I learned to make in Japan and really enjoyed preparing for her. Because Rachel was so capable, intellegent, and lovely, she was pursued by many suitors, which I found very stressful. It is always difficult to watch young loved ones become independent but also occassionaly get hurt, which inevitably happens. Balancing my desires to see her grow while also protecting her is a struggle every parent faces.

My daughters all attended my 55th birthday on February 25th. Sarah was wanting to talk about her upcoming marriage to Allan. I conveyed to her that I would do all I could to make it a wonderful wedding.

Shortly after my birthday, on March 5th, I had a dream. I went to a place called, "Land of Self." It was similar to how one might imagine heaven, in other words, *anima mundi* (or "world soul"). Historically, the concept of *anima mundi* is related to the balance between universal mind (*animus dei*) and universal soul. The relation between these two can be characterized through the relation between active and passive, which require one another to create and sustain life. When I woke up I had the feeling of awe and the freedom of ultimate peace. And then I thought, "It's real! The truth shall set you free!"

At this time, I had a relationship with a very nice and caring woman, though we had slight incompatibilities. For example, she was very extroverted, and gained much joy from being out and with her many dear friends, whereas I'm introverted and became a bit exhausted. I finally took a tally of the relationship when it became clear that she wanted to get married. However, because of the pain of the betrayal and divorce, I was leery of doing that again. So this woman and I separated. Afterward she seemed to flourish and I felt much relief, even writing in my journal that every breakthrough starts with a break. This breakup also happened during spring break, which lead to my musing about the connections between breaking off and breaking up, breaking out and breaking through.

Despite the pain that always accompanies ending a relationship, our decision to separate felt renewing for us both. This new opening in my life gave me the mental space and energy to throw myself into teaching and research again. I was reminded just how much I love leading a classroom and creating meaning in academic settings.

For example, one of the joys of my time in academia was chairing my own research team. Out of that team, Randy Arnau became a lead author on a paper about measuring personality types. We were happy it was accepted by *The Journal of Analytical Psychology*, the premier journal regarding Jung's psychology.

I have a fondness for Taoism, and have had for many years. So this spiritual interest has worked its way into my research. For example, one of the undergraduates on our research team, Ellen Crouse, requested to study wisdom and Taoism. What resulted from that was a fascinating study of the integration of Taoism and the psychologies of Carl Jung, Eric Erikson, and Abraham Maslow. We found that these psychologies are all quite similar in the culmination of individuation, self-realization, and self-actualization. We wrote a paper together, "The Tao of Wisdom: Ingegration of Taoism and the psychologies of Jung, Erikson, and Maslow" which was published in a book entitled, *Pschology of Mature Spirituality.*

This orientation toward Taoism also found its way into my medical writing and practice. For instance, "The Tao of Medicine" was published in the medical journal, *The Pharos.* The purpose of the article was to show that wholistic healing involves hope, will, trust, purpose, competency, fidelity, love, care, and wisdom. This was an extension of Eric Erikson's theory of personality.
I gave a related lecture at my Alma Mater, "Physcian, Heal Thyself and The Tao of Medicine," The University of Missouri. Later, a graduate student working with me, Michael Luebbert, did his research on forgivness. He tought me a great deal. Randy Arnau and myself were delighted to contribute to this research, culminating in a presentation at the American Psychological Association Annual Meeting entitled, "Predicting Forgiveness Success from Maladaptive Schemas, Aattachment, and Psychosocial Resolution."

Later that same year I gave talks in Boulder, Colorado and Kansas City, Missouri on "The Soul of Haiku." These lectures were the result of my time in Japan. They were usually given at Jungian societies were open to the public and therefore drew a varied audience.

An additional area of interest is how to use art in the healing process. This theme is actually interwoven with all of my work. The art therapy program at Naropa University in Boulder Colorado invited me to give a lecture because of the way healing through art was presented in *Transforming Depression.*

In August of this year, I gave grand rounds in a case conference at Texas Tech University in Lubbock Texas. Randy Schiffer, who had invited me, had been a colleague at Rochester, before becoming department head at the Texas Tech Medical school. In addition to having a lovely time at the talks, Randy and I had several meals together and it was wonderful to catch up.

Toward the end of the year, I had a dream of Elvis. He was alive and well. I had an old, classic white car and he liked it. Elvis wanted to sit and talk, so we did. He even gave me his telephone number. I was searching for a spiritual book to show him, but I couldn't find it. I said I would send it to him later, since I had his address. He was the young Elvis, kind and friendly. I was in my 40s and we all lived in Beverly Hills.

Shortly after this dream, all the talks I had given about Elvis began to crystalize into a book, a pyschological and philosophical study of his life. I began writing the book in 2000, though it would not be published until 2002.

December 30th of 2000 was a big day, because my eldest daughter Sarah got married to Allan. The wedding was lovely and went extremely well. My ex-wife even congratulated us on the wonderful job we had done with Sarah. Sarah and I danced at the reception to "My Father's Eyes" and Allan danced with his mother to the song, "It's a Wonderful World." And indeed it was a wonderful world that night, and such a lovely way to round out the year.

Chapter 20: A Taste for Detail

"What memory has in common with art is the knack for selection,
the taste for detail...memory contains precisely details, not the whole
picture, highlights, if you will, not the entire show."

—JOSEPH BRODSKY[1]

Flowing down the river with a man.

This is all I remember of this dream. But even tiny dream fragments are important, because they offer clues to what is happening
in your unconscious. In this case, I am going down the river of
life with my shadow (who is the same sex person in a dream, i.e.
men will have male shadows). This got me recalling a book I had
recently read called *Flow,* by Mihaly Csikszentmihalyi, the essence
of which was that one needs to look at and accept ones life and the
meaning it provides. This leads to self-acceptance. As Brodsky's
quote notes, memories tend to come in fragments and details, but
remembering the hologram, even a part of one's life does represent
the whole. As Jung maintained, meaning involves a tension of the
opposites.

1. Joseph Brodsky was a Russian born, Nobel prize winning poet and es-
sayist expelled from the Soviet Union in 1972.

In February of 2001 I dreamt I was making love with a former highschool girflriend, a Belgium exchange student named Marÿke. This is vital in that I'm embracing my anima, the feminine part of myself. For a man, integrating this part of oneself is vital to self-understanding.

As a 56 year old father, I accepted a challenge from my youngest daughter, Rachel, to go on a cruise to Jamaica with her and two of her teenage friends (I called the three of them the *tres amigas*). Of course Laura, my middle daughter, also wanted to go. Since she was in between a wild adolescent and an adult, she was indispensible in helping her father deal with three teenage girls on a Caribbean cruise. I will always remember that trip and her presence there fondly.

Traveling
with teens
glimpses of growing up

On our way to the cruise departure in Florida, we visited my aunts Ruth and Esta Rosen, and their husbands, Saul and George. Ruth and Esta were identical twins, and were going to be 84 in March of that year. As little girls, they were in an early silent film. We had the loveliest time.

I noted in a journal on March 14th of 2001 that it was a very quiet day at sea, which I spent sunning on the deck and grading papers. If one must grade papers, that is a lovely place to do it. The ship toured Cozumel, Jamaica, Belize, and Grand Cayman Island. They were all extrordinary locations, but Grand Cayman Island was as close to perfect as it's possible to be. It was so nice to rest there on our journey. In Belize we stopped at Georgetown, a port with clear water and it was absolutely gorgeous. However the *tres amigas* were more interested in finding a Subway Sandwhich than the beaches, so they took off while Laura and I hung out at the magnificent coast.

The next stop: Jamaica. We arrived early in the morning and went only on one tour, to Dunn's Falls. I had actually been to these falls before, when, as a 14 year old, I went on an ill-fated cruise with my family from Miami to the Carribbean and we got caught in a hurricane. Dunn's falls are spectacular and the girls and I got super wet, although we had a ton of fun. In the afternoon, Laura and I went to a local craft market and met the three girls there. The crafts and artwork were superb, if very much underpriced given their obvious craftsmanship. I bought Rachel a woodcarving for her upcoming birthday (in April), and bought myself a rockwood carving of a woman's head. Laura got lots of necklaces and bracelets, as well as carvings. The market was packed with people, and I thanked the supreme being that the girls made it back to the ship safe and sound. Another gift I got for folks was Jamaican coffee.

The girls were well behaved almost the entire trip, but there was one incident that gave me pause. I recall knocking (loudly and insessantly) on the door of the room Rachel shared with her friends. The door opened slowly and clouds of smoke came billowing out that I knew was marijuana. There sat the three girls, alongside three teenage boys I'd never seen before, smoking joints. The boys looked as shocked as I was, and they left quickly, leaving the girls to enjoy their pot and me to plot (how I should keep a closer eye on those three).

On St. Patrick's day we were back at sea, and we saw a school of flying fish as we passed Cuba. That night, to deal with the stress of a tumultous sea, Laura and I hit the black jack table (well, Laura just watched me). I don't usually gamble, but I did manage to win $50.

We arrived back in the states in mid march, but even on land I kept dreaming about being on a ship. Alas, vacations must end, and I had to ready myself for the first week of a class I developed on Psychology of Religion for honors students.

At the end of the March I went to the annual Fay lectures, which were delivered by Brazilian analyist Roberto Gambini on "Soul and Culture." They were exceptionally good. Roberto's first Fay lecture, "Soulmaking and the New World" was an insightful talk about the history of how partriachal Europe, via the Portugese, subjugated the brazilian indigenous peoples by raping native women and the environment. And while I'm writing this, the Amazon is burning due to mismanagement, so capitalist colonialism is still violating the earth.

As I've mentioned, I loved to cook for my daughters. I made vegetable soup on a regular basis, and even eventually got to include that in my humorous cookbook, "The Alchemy of Cooking:

Recipes with a Jungian Twist." The cookbook includes recipes for such illustrious favorites as anima eggs and animus bacon, and the individuated omlette. Thomas Moore admits in his foreword, that there are very few references to Jung in the cookbook, but he has a special comment about my inclusion of a recipe for a peanut butter and jelly sandwhich.

Speaking of cooking, at Thanksgiving, all three daughters came home, and Sarah brought her husband Allan and Rachel brought her boyfriend Craig. We made so much food that we even made two kinds of pie, including Aunt Bessie's pecan pie. We all ate too much. In fact, I even wrote in my journal that "I felt unbalanced."

Thanksgiving night I dreamt I was by myself near a sea on a six month fellowship. This is prophetic, since only a few years later I was to take a 7 month sabbatical at the University of Canterbury in Christchurch, where I would meet Lanara. We lived in seperate abodes in Govorners Bay on the south island. I didn't realize at the time how important Alfred Lord Tennyson's poem was in my life,

> *I hold it true, whate'er befall;*
> *I feel it, when I sorrow most;*
> *'Tis better to have loved and lost*
> *Than never to have loved at all.*

My first marriage was exciting, like a roller coaster ride. My second marriage provided three wonderful daughters, and my third marriage, forthcoming in the last chapter, proved the maxim "The third time is the charm."

Chapter 21: Retreat In a Monastary

Truth is like the sun. You can shut it out for a time, but it ain't goin' away.

—ELVIS PRESLEY

I hear a voice that tells me, "You're going to be alone tomorrow." My ex, Debbie, asks Rachel, "Do you want to come with me" and Rachel went with her, even though she looked sad.

This was a dream that was in part a reworking of my second divorce. Dreaming of Debbie meant that I needed to forgive her and go on with my life. In other words, my negative mother complex was being analyzed to death. Regarding the voice, sometimes one hears things in dreams. It's unusual, but it happens. This was a prophetic voice, telling me I was in need of, and was going to take, a needed respite this year. The following haiku, which I wrote early in the year, contains a seed of what I hoped to experience in getting away.

Village of thatched roofs
On a lush mountain
The monk's meal of greens[1]

1. Rosen, David. (2002) Modern Haiku 33.2, 39.

Chapter 21: Retreat In a Monastary

This year was filled with many blessings, including the release of a new book, the birth of my first grandchild, and a much needed stay at a monastary in Pecos, New Mexico.

The accomplishment of a new book, *The Tao of Elvis*, was a positive feeling. The fact that the first edition came out with a major publisher was particularly rewarding. But it was also very exhausting. Harcourt Press had arranged for me to do a book tour all over the U.S., for example Memphis, Miami, New Orleans, and the place where I did much of my growing up, Springfield, Missouri.

THE TAO OF ELVIS

"The Tao is great, the king is also great."
—LAO TZU

DAVID ROSEN

On March 9th, 2002, Aidan Noah was born, my first grandchild. His birth was quite difficult, so we were relieved everyone was healthy. Shakespeare was right, "All is well that ends well." It's hard to believe that as I write this, Aidan is ready to go to college. He is a gifted young man, with huge creative potential. I've often thought he would make a great author or playwright. In fact, whatever he ends up doing he will excell.

After a tiring book tour, and a hectic, exciting time around Aidan's birth, I was ready for some rest and relaxation. So I headed to Pecos, New Mexico for a silent retreat at Our Lady of Guadalupe Monastery. I arranged to have a hermitage, so that I could be entirely by myself. The grounds of this monestary are beautiful. There is a trail that follows a river, and it is just you and nature. You are left alone by the monks and nuns, but also served simple food alongside them at meal times. The following series of haiku were written at the Pecos Abbey.

The first haiku is entitled, "Hosana Madona." While walking along the path near the Pecos River there was a tree, about 12' high, in which a monk had carved an image of a smiling and strong mother with her arms around her child.

> Mother and child
> Eternal thanks-
> Water flows

The next haiku were inspired by the natural beauty.

> Three crows
> Ride cold winds-
> Our Lady immovable under the pines

> I am
> No more than flowing water

Chapter 21: Retreat In a Monastary

No more than sunny skies
No more than howling wind

By the river's edge
Music of the soul-
Birds sing along

Walking back to the Abbey
Trees bowing to the river
I feel the same way

Affirmation that the experience was healing occured in the month when I returned. It was a lovely day and I was out on the deck at my home toward the end of April. I was journaling and I felt blessed.

I received a shipment of *The Tao of Elvis* books from Harcourt. Like May Sarton once said, "We author's write books to give them away," something I also embody. In the published book, the dedicaiton is for my youngest daughter, and it reads, "For Rachel and her Song of Songs." Naturally I gave Rachel her own copy, in which I hand wrote a more personal dedication.

During Rachel's transition to college I focused on a lot of self-care. As was (and still is) typical, I received regular massages. This helped me to be centered and relaxed, and I recommend it for others.

At the end of April, I had a fun party for around 20 people. I invited all my Ph.D. students, members of my research team, and even other grads who were not my students. I made a bunch of cheese enchiladas, and folks brought other food so we ended up with a big pot luck dinner. This party, like many others, was very rewarding. We had a lovely time, and a couple students even stayed to clean up and help with the dishes. Academia can be so difficult and boring, so it's important to build community where you can. I have never forgotten that I, too, am a student.

In May of 2002, I headed to San Antonio for the Inter-Regional Society of Jungian Analysts. I talked to my friend and colleague, Clarissa Pinkola Estes, who wrote the powerful book, *Women Who Run with the Wolves*. We always supported one another in our creative and other efforts.

In the summer, I traveled to England, where I gave several presentations at the First International Academic Conference of Analytical Psychology, at University of Essex in Colchester, England. I took two graduate students with me—Nathan Mascaro and Randy Arnau, both of whom also gave talks at the conference. It was a delight to watch them flourish in this academic setting.

Next I traveled to Vancouver, Canada, where an undergraduate student and my god daughter, Anahita Varahami, was selected to give a talk at an international conference on Personal Meaning. She did great and made me very proud.

The end of the year was spent giving presentations on *The Tao of Elvis*, in Louisiana, Texas, Georgia, Pennsylvania, and Alabama. I very much enjoyed these presentations, although by this time in the year I was also exhausted. Still, it is nice to see one's work get such positive and wide reception.

Toward the end of 2002, I had a dream in which one woman shot another with a pistol on a harrowing journey. This dream indicates that my anima, my inner woman, took on and killed her double. This most likely reflects the process of working through the divorce and other difficult, past relationships, and also letting go of my negative mother complex.

Chapter 22: The Healing Spirit of Haiku

As I travel through my life
Times of joy and times of strife
I pray now to realize
The whole within-energize
My spirit self to align
With Universal All Divine

BEVERLY SHAPIRO

If you wanted to, you could write history in Haiku.

H. W. BRANDS

I dreamt that my nephew Jonathan Meyer was with me and he was taking a shower without soap. He was asking for soap and I gave him some.

This dream fragment points to how my shadow was being cleansed and reborn, in a kind of baptism. I've always felt close to Jonathan, as we both love to paint, and people have said we are very similar, both in looks and philosophy.

Santa Chiara Campus

The City of Castiglion Fiorentino

One of the benefits of being a faculty member at Texas A&M University was the fact that they had a campus called Santa Chiara, in Castiglion Fiorentino, Tuscany, Italy. To start out the 2003 year, I spent an entire semester teaching at that gorgeous campus. The courses I taught were very meaningful to me and to the students. I taught "Psychology of Religion," which allowed me to take the students to visit all manner of religious places, such as the path walked by St. Francis of Assisi, the monestary and chappel Francis frequented in Assisi, and other places. The history of the Santa Chiara campus is also interesting religiously. As you may know, St. Clare was an intimate friend and religious comrade of St. Francisis of Assisi, and this was originally her nunnery (purchased and turned into a university campus by Texas A&M). It is such a stunning magical place all year round, even though it would occassionally snow. But the beauty of the city was undimmed, in fact, it was highlighted, by the snow.

Snow in Castiglion Florentino

remarkable. . .

worth remembering

Convento de le Celle

In the spring I visited Convento de le Celle, in Cortona, the monastary where Francis spent the majority of his service to God in his monastic cell. It was one of the most stunning places I have ever been. It was clearly a sacred and remote location.

Also, while at Santa Chiara, I taught "Psychology of Self," which was about each individual's personal myth. In other words, I would ask the students, "Why are you here? What is your purpose?" This was very deep for the students (and painful, for some), but it was a very moving, existential journey for all of us and to this day I rememer the class very, very fondly.

Once, while traveling on a train to Rome to visit the Vatican and other special sites, I met a woman serendipidously named Mimi Rosenwasser. Her father was a German Jew, who fled to Alsace Lorraine during WWII, and her mother was born and raised Catholic. Mimi was the name of the nanny who cared for me from birth until age two, and Rosenwasser (literally water of roses) is very close to my own last name, Rosen (roses). Because it was valentines day, I offered to take her to a lovely meal. After that, I wrote the following haiku.

> Happy Valentine's
> Rosenwasser glistening. . .
> two ducks together.

I visited Rome several times while staying in Tuscany. I especially loved the Sistine Chapel at the Vatican. I marvelled at the beauty, of course, but also the technique and mastery needed to paint that enormous ceiling with such perfect perspective.

I also visited Capri—I took a train to Sorrento and hopped on a ferry to get to Capri and the Blue Grotto. Both places are stunning; you just don't forget going to places this magnificent. I drew the following sketch of my journey from Serrento to Capri.

Journey to Capri

While at Santa Chiara, the students were offered a sculpting class with Alberto Bruni. I was delighted to find out that faculty could also take courses. I had never sculpted before, but really enjoyed the experience. I made the stone mandala pictured below.

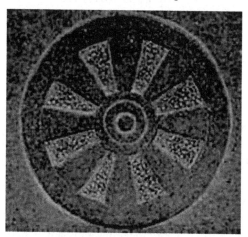

Stone mandala carved in Italy

My daughters Rachel and Laura visted me in Santa Chiara, and we had the chance to take a trip to Venice together with the students. While there, we went to a restaraunt named Madona and had dinner with the president of Texas A&M, who happened to be visiting the Italian campus. To our amazement, he paid for the entire meal for everyone. Later, we went to Peggy Guggenheim's former home, which she had turned into a museum at her death. It was incredible: with works from the greats, including Degas, Chagall, Rembrant and others.

I also went to Corfu, Greece to visit my friend and colleague, Anthony Stevens, who lives on this beautiful island. I remember fondly his lovely home and the conversations we had. I also recall a walk we took through olive groves by the coast, which prompted me to write the following two haiku in my journal.

Sun on sea
swaying bamboo
bay of sculpted cliffs

Walk through olive groves
a peaceful silence. . .
wildflowers everywhere

Sometimes a dream does not need interpretation. The day I flew home to the U.S. I had a dream that I was in Italy being my creative self. Goodbye Italy.

Coming home from trips is often difficult. Catching up and going through stacks of mail is never easy. Pretty soon I found myself right back in boring faculty meetings and Santa Chiara felt like a dream.

I needed some help acclimating to the stress of work and a relationship that I was in. Being a psychoanalyst, I am quite used to seeking help for myself when needed. At the time, I started seeing my first (and only) Kleinian analytic therapist. Her name was Marsha McCary, and she followed the object relations theory of Melanie Klein. She was very helpful to me in many ways. Specifically, in regards to a relationship I was in at the time, she said to me, "David, the woman are with is like your mother. And that's dangerous. Leave that relationship." I was at first stunned, but once I thought about it, I knew she was right. I felt I had been a failure in my work and marriages, but she really helped me acept myself and my gifts.

Despite feeling overwhelmed by retuning to work (teaching, research, and seeing patients), I had missed my home and community. My house was at the end of a cul de sac called Brazoswood, with a lovely backyard and deck. While sitting outside one day, grateful to be home, I wrote these poems.

Wind blows
Sun shines
Birds call-
What else is there?

Sitting by jasmine
Fragrance of spring. . .
Two fireflies appear

I used to sit out on the deck, eat breakfast, and listen to the birds. I especially loved the cardinals. This haiku emerged from one of those moments.

Small miracle
Leonardo da Vinci
set caged birds free

I learned, when visiting da Vinci's home in Italy, that he would go to the market and buy birds stuck in cages in order to set them free. So, in a nice way, all that I learned and felt in Italy was brought home with me, and still present even as I sat listening to birds on my deck thousands of miles a way.

In the Autumn, I dreamt that I had a close friendship with a woman of African descent. Both Jewish and African American individuals have a history of enslavement. In this dream, through the friendship, I was overcoming my own dislike of my inner self and accepting my discriminated, feminine anima. In other words I was loving myself.

At this time, Rachel invited me to a father-daughter banquet and dance at Austin College in Sherman, Texas, which she attended. We had a lovely time and she was so interested in and excited about her classes, and thrilled to be at that school. I was honored she would share that experience with me.

That holiday season, Rachel came home. On New Years Eve, we painted together on the deck. As you can see, Rachel's mandala (picture below) is about the tension of the opposites, water and fire. My mandala, which is pictured at the front of this book (and titled moving toward wholeness), has the same theme. That night I had a dream of making mandalas out of pieces. I guess that's a pretty obvious and auspicious sign about the direciton of my life.

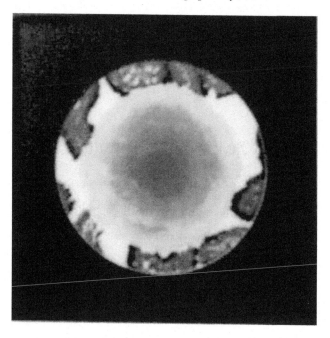

Chapter 23: Existential Meaning—2004

Who knows this morning what will happen tonight?

—CHINESE PROVERB

Interestingly, 2004 started out with more St. Francsis of Assis. Although this time, I was visiting Santa Fe, New Mexico. The city's full legal name remains *La Villa Real de la Santa Fe de San Francisco de Asisi* (the royal town of the holy faither of Saint Francis of Assisi). I had arranged to spend a few days with a friend and colleague, and fellow Jungian analyist. We were very fond of each other, and had spent two years enjoying each other's company and traveling together. Uncortunately, as with other women I had been with, I was still uncertain about commitment and so we amicably parted ways.

I was, however, in the midst of other forms of healing. For example I was working a very exciting project, "The Healing Spirit of Haiku" with my longest term friend, Joel Weishaus. The book came out in 2004, to our great delight.

THE
Healing Spirit
OF
Haiku

David Rosen *&* Joel Weishaus
with illustrations by ARTHUR OKAMURA

We were lucky to have a talented artist, Arthur Okamura, illustrate many haiku throughout the book. He was a friend of Joel's from prior projects. The cover image was inspired by the following haiku.

> Shimmering patty
> The slap of small feet nearing
> Where dragonflies hover

In a subsequent letter to Joel, also fond of haiku, I reflected on my motivations for writing such poems and my own creative process. I wrote two different versions of the following short poem, and I even gave Joel an explanation of why I changed and added things in the second version.

> Walking
> past an electric angel. . .
> moon appears

Walking
passed an electric angel. . .
blue moon appears.

Don't know why I put "past" for "passed" in the first poem and left out blue. Maybe it had to do with the end of my recent relationship. Or maybe because a lot of my past had been blue. I was considering giving up depression: not darkness or sadness, but just depression, as I feel that these are intimately tied to creativity. I had been working on this part of my journey since publishing "Transforming Depression."

Because of the recent publication, I gave a number of talks about this new work at Jung institutes in various places. Then I met Joel in Portland, where he lived, and we gave a talk together at the Japenese Garden.

Also this year, a graduate student of mine, Nathan Mascaro, developed a Spiritual Meaning Scale, under the guidance of myself and Les Morey (a fellow proffessor at Texas A&M). This scale measures how spiritual someone is, asking them questions about how they relate to the universe, how it was formed and how they reflect on their own path, etc. In other words, it is not a religious scale. The point of this scale is to be able to measure someone's (or your own) spirituality. It could be used and interpreted in a lot of ways, but as a Jungian, the significance of the scale for me had more to with indicating how individuated and healthy one is, and how they relate to wholeness.

I continued to work with Nathan on a number of projects, including one about the role of existential meaning and its role in the enhancement of hope and the prevention of depressive symptoms. We published a paper on this together, in the Jounral of Personality.

At this time I was in a process where the Deans office was reviewing my professorship. Often these processes are very stressful, but

I found my own experience very rewarding. Because the head of my department had not wanted to give me a salary increase, I had to make an appeal to the associate provost's office. Grievances are a big part of academic life, and though filing them against one's department can be challenging, it's sometimes necessary. In this case, it really paid off. Rather than recommending zero increase, the provost's office recommended a full 10% increase.

At the end of the year, I was in Pittsburgh to lead a Jungian workshop for people in training to be analysts. I enjoyed the city and the surround very much. I suppose because Pittsburgh had been known as a steel city—industrial and dark—I was especially surprised to find that it was very bright, artistic, and intellectual. My experience there inspired the follow haiku:

Sun breaks through gray sky
birches before everygreens
ligh snow falls

Deer graze
horses stay put
clouds appear, dissapear

At this time, my eldest daughter Sarah and her husband Allan were raising their growing family College Station, Texas. It was nice to be so close to them. They would later move to Spicewood, in the Austin area, when Sarah pursued her dream of having a center for abused children, which she set up nearby in Marble Falls. It's called the Phoenix Center and it was an extraordinary feeling when her dream came true. She worked hard, but that's what it takes to actualize one's vision. Being in the rural area of Spicewood allowed them to enjoy the beauty, the tall cedar trees, and the lakes, which are so important for growing kids and for spiritual health in general.

As I've aged, I've grown to share Sarah and Allan's desire to settle into a lovely place, and become one with nature. I sensed they were moving that direction and it made me feel so good for their kids. When I was young, I traveled and moved and was always in search of the divine out and about, but I have settled down and find peace closer to home. I am reminded of a quote by Epicurus, "It is not the young man who should be considered fortunate but the old man who has lived well, because the young man in his prime wanders much by chance, vacillating in his beliefs, while the old man has docked in the harbor, having safeguarded his true happiness."

The spider web
mysterious spiral
life and death[1]

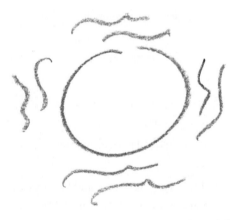

This drawing grew out of feeling balanced, and my delight in Sarah and her happiness.

1. Rosen, D.H. (2013). *Clouds and More Clouds*. Northfield, MA: Lily Pool Press.

Chapter 24: Meeting My Soul Mate—2005

Two solitudes protect, touch, and greet each other.

—RILKE

I went to New Zealand to write a memoir, *Lost in the Long White Cloud: Finding My Way Home*. As I have mentioned before, I thought that I would never want to get married again. After two divorces, I avoided long-term relationships. Nearly all the women I was with wanted to get married. But, I got used to saying no.

This was the case until I met Lanara on a bench in New Zealand. We were both living in Governors Bay on the South Island, and destiny brought us together. In my youth, I was an exchange student in Greece, and always wanted to return there to live on an island. It's synchronicity, therefore, that Lanara has Greek roots. So, in a way, Greece came to me when I met her on a different island in the Pacific.

I went to a park, Allendale, where I often ate lunch. I would then walk on the foreshore down to the jetty. I was surprised to see a lovely woman on the bench I usually sat on. I'm not being facetious when I say that it was love at first sight. It really was. I went up to her and asked, "Excuse me, would you mind if I sat here and ate my lunch?" She said, "No, that's fine." I got out the apple packed in my lunch and asked if she would like half of it. She agreed and I gave it to her. It turned out that she was walking back to the jetty where I was going and her car was parked there, so we walked together.

Jetty at Governors Bay

Governors Bay

It would take us four years to decide to get married. I wanted this far more than she did at first, as I proposed to her in the Qantas line when I was leaving New Zealand in 2005, only four months after having met her. So much for not wanting to get married again.

I went back to New Zealand two times after meeting Lanara. The third time, she agreed to return with me to Texas, so I danced for hours within. My heart was light and bright. Nevertheless, and fortunately, Lanara did not like the Lone Star state.

Over the course of our time together, we often talked about settling down at the end of a gravel road in a forested area. Flashing forward, in 2008, we decided to house-sit in Eugene, Oregon. We fell in love with the town and surround. Eventially, Lanara found the perfect piece of property at the end of a lane. We bought the land and built a small house there. In other words, our dream came true. As Lao Tzu maintained, "Nature does not hurry, yet everything is accomplished."

Anyway, back to my time in New Zealand. While there, I had the opportunity to go on New Zealand's national radio and be interviewed by the formidable Kim Hill. Not having had a radio, I didn't really understand the import of being interviewed by her. Actually, I was even running a little late, and didn't think anything of it. It turned out that the show was really popular, Kim was a fantastic interviewer, and it was a wonderful experience. She was really down to earth. We talked mostly about *Transforming Depression* and *The Tao of Jung*, and made plans to discuss *The Tao of Elvis* at a future date. Kim was especially intrigued by the interviews I conducted with ten people who had jumped off of the Golden Gate Bridge and lived, each of whom recounted having spiritual experiences on their way down. We speculated about the import of these experiences in their healing process. Fortuitously, Kim was also a fan of Jung's. The conversation was very stimulating, grounded, and mature.

At the end of 2005, though sad to leave Lanara, New Zealand, and the friends and colleagues I met there, I was excited to return to Texas A&M for a special art show on Mandalas and Floral Meditiatons. In conjunction with students from the Institute for Floral Design at Texas A&M, I put on an art show that thematized the relationship between mandalas and floral design. I contributed several of my own paintings or other art I'd gathered over the years. Each student then selected one and created a floral design that spoke to the themes, colors, and images in the original art. They wrote stunning reflections, discussing how the mandalas spoke to them, and how they brought forth their own creation. The students were incredibly creative, and brilliant artists all. It was a very meaningful experience. In the example below, artist Kristen Atnipp selected and created a piece inspired by the stone mandala that I made in Italy (and pictured above). She chose this mandala because it reminded her of her chosen field, horticulture, in part because the image is reminiscent of a flower, which brought her peace.

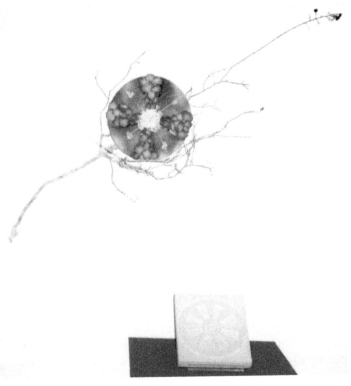

Chapter 24: Meeting My Soul Mate—2005

As I bring this second volume of my memoir to a close, I realize that my nature is that of an artist. As a kid, I had the sense about myself that I would be a farmer and an artist. I managed to become an artist all by myself, but it took meeting and marrying Lanara before I could actualize the farming part of myself. It's skipping ahead somewhat, but Lanara and I would eventually marry in 2009. I discovered the truth of the old adage, "Third time's the charm." In fact, there's maybe something special about the number three—the trinity. This is my second of three memoirs, my third wife is my soulmate, and I have three beautiful, creative, and intelligent daughters. In fact, it's maybe appropriate to end this memoir with a reflection on them, since they are so much a part of me.

They have accomplished so much. Sarah founded The Phoenix Center, a non-profit that helps inspire hope, health, and healing in abused or neglected children by providing mental health care and trauma-informed therapy to them and their families. She is 43 and married to Allan, a judge, and they have two amazing sons, Aidan and Ben. They are dear grandsons and what a joy it is! Laura is 38 and has a terrific career working for a humanist pediatrician who is very involved in social justice. She has a background in finance, and also worked hard to set up programs that help children and families save money for the future, like when she worked with the Center for Public Policy Priorities and Opportunity Texas. She and her partner Paul live in Austin. Rachel (35) has an education in leadership from Stanford, and works as an educational consultant. Sensing a need for improved communication across differences, she founded S.P.A.R.K., a fun and meaningful card game that builds empathy with others and raises awareness of how one's identity impacts their expeirence. She also now lives Austin, with her partner, Lia.

I feel lucky to have three daughters who are so ultruistic, committed to serving their communities, and to making the world a better place. I agree with Lao Tsu, that there are just three things to teach:

simplicity, patience, and compassion. It's fortuante that Lanara and my daughters have all three of these traits in abundance.

In finishing this part of my autobiography, I am happy to have a chance to step back from the hard work of reveiwing my life required by this memoir, and to return to the creative things I'm enjoying these days, like painting, writing poetry, and living quietly in nature. I'm hoping to now embody the ninth chapter of the Tao Te Ching, which advises that we each do our work and then step back, which is the only path to serenity.

The journey is the reward

—Taoist saying

Lanara and I in New Zealand

Chapter 25: Final Reflection

Life after death. . .an interesting possibility, especially as you age. Now, clearly old aged (being seventy five), it is quite appealing. However, I and others just don't know. Even my Hindu friends are not convincing. And, what's wrong with death anyway? There must also be death after death. But, given my love for Lanara, I'd like to be with her in the next realm. Also, when my daughters and their loved ones pass, I'd like to see and be with them , my grandsons, and my beloved k9 companions. Is that wish-fulfillment or reality?

Nevertheless, I want to be buried in a simple wooden box in the earth on our property. In fact, I'd like to be interned between a willow tree, where Willow's ashes are buried, and a magnolia tree, where my mother's ashes are. Our second Willow (which was her given name when we adopted her, though we changed it to Willa) will also join us. It's clear we love our dogs. Nobody wants to outlive their partner, and that is how Lanara and I feel. But fate will determine that. However, it is well known that women outlive men. If that is true, then she'll be around a lot longer than myself.

Willow

Willa

Lanara has created an arboretum where we live. We have planned for a family and retreat center for artists and writers. We also plan to apply for a conservation easement, which, if granted, would ensure that our thirty acres with three trails would never be developed. It will be an oasis in nature for one to be their true personal being and to be with the Supreme Being. Our place is ideal for rest, relaxation, and creativity. It is peaceful and feels sacred. We see our abode as an island of serenity in a sea of fast-paced chaos. It will always be a source of creative quietude. In front of our house is a real frog pond with those little creatures often serenading us and future residents. They love to sing their ribbits in late fall, winter, and spring, during and after the rainy season.

Lanara is a dear soul of nature and our mutual love has turned out well. Then we set our sights on "weller than well." This marriage and building our home and living at the end of Camas lane has allowed us to actualize dreams. We plan to leave our place as a center this for family and other individuals to actualize their creative potential. This makes our hearts sing and our souls rejoice.

One of my favorite books is *The Sorrows of Young Werther* by Johann Wolfgang von Goethe. It was his first novel, written in 1774. I remember reading this incredible book when I was a college student. My life and my books about egocide and creative transformation are related, so I feel a kinship with Goethe. His important novel is about a relationship gone sour, which was autobiographical. The protagonist converts his pain and anguish into a creative and lasting saga. So, we welcome future families and others to play, enjoy, heal, and create at our place.

Appendix

Connecting with South Africa: Cultural Communication and Understanding
Berg, Astrid (Texas A&M University Press, 2012)

Finding Jung
McMillan, Frank N. (Texas A&M University Press, 2012)

The Therapeutic Relationship: Transference, Countertransference, and the Making of Meaning
Wiener, Jan (Texas A&M University Press, 2009)

Synchronicity: Nature and Psyche in an Interconnected Universe
Cambray, Joseph (Texas A&M University Press, 2009)

Ethics and Analysis: Philosophical Perspectives and Their Application in Therapy
Zoja, Luigi (Texas A&M University Press, 2007)

Memories of Our Lost Hands: Searching for Feminine Spirituality and Creativity
Toyoda, Sonoko (Texas A&M University Press, 2006)

The Black Sun: the Alchemy and Art of Darkness
Marlan, Stanton (Texas A&M University Press, 2005)

Soul and Culture
Gambini, Roberto (Texas A&M University Press, 2003)

The Old Woman's Daughter
Douglas, Claire (Texas A&M University Press, 2006)

The Stillness Shall Be the Dancing
Woodman, Marion (Texas A&M University Press, 1994)

Gender and Desire: Uncursing Pandora
Young-Eisendrath, Polly (Texas A&M University Press, 1997)

The Two Million-Year-Old Self
Stevens, Anthony (Texas A&M University Press, 1993)

Buddhism and the art of Psychotherapy
Kawai, Hayao (Texas A&M University Press, 1996)

Joy, Inspiration and Hope
Kast, Verena (Texas A&M University Press, 1991)

Integrity in Depth
Beebe, John (Texas A&M University Press, 1992)

The Archetypal Imagination
Hollis, James (Texas A&M University Press, 2000)

Transformation: emergence of the self
Stein, Murray (Texas A&M University Press, 1998)

The Soul of Art: Analysis and creation
Christian Caillard (Texas A&M University Press, 2017)

Madness and Creativity
Ann Belford Ulanov (Texas A&M University Press, 2013)

Appendix

Brothers and Sisters: Myth and reality
Henry Abramovitch (Texas A&M University Press, 2014).